BEYOND THE BROWSER

BEYOND THE BROWSER

Web 2.0 and Librarianship

Karl Bridges

LIBRARIES UNLIMITED

AN IMPRINT OF ABC-CLIO, LLC
Santa Barbara, California • Denver, Colorado • Oxford, England

Library of Congress Cataloging-in-Publication Data

Bridges, Karl, 1964–
  Beyond the browser : Web 2.0 and librarianship / Karl Bridges.
    p. cm.
  Includes bibliographical references and index.
  ISBN 978–1–59158–816–0 (pbk.) — ISBN 978–1–59158–817–7 (ebook)
1. Libraries and the Internet. 2. Librarians—Effect of technological innovations on.
3. Web 2.0. I. Title.
Z674.75.I58B75   2012
020.285′4678—dc23   2011043074

ISBN: 978–1–59158–816–0
EISBN: 978–1–59158–817–7

16 15 14 13 12   1 2 3 4 5

This book is also available on the World Wide Web as an eBook.
Visit www.abc-clio.com for details.

Libraries Unlimited
An Imprint of ABC-CLIO, LLC

ABC-CLIO, LLC
130 Cremona Drive, P.O. Box 1911
Santa Barbara, California 93116-1911

This book is printed on acid-free paper ∞

Manufactured in the United States of America

Copyright Acknowledgments
Karl Bridges, "Boyd Cycle Theory in the Context of Non-Cooperative Games: Implications for Libraries," *Library Philosophy and Practice*, Vol. 6, No. 2 (Spring 2004), reprinted with permission.

Karl Bridges, "Librarians and the Attention Economy," *Library Philosophy and Practice* (2008), reprinted with permission.

For Rita my lovely wife and Jane my awesome godmother

Contents

Introduction

The genesis of this book came years ago when I was talking with a university administrator who told me he had just authorized $1 million worth of technology purchases—and this was not at my present institution, mind you. "On what?" I asked. And he replied: "I have no idea. The technology people just showed up and told me if I didn't agree to it the university would collapse." This was, I would note, neither a stupid nor foolish administrator, but, rather, one known for his steely-eyed consideration of the budget.

Unfortunately, based on my 20 years of experience in academia, I suspect that the situation confronting that administrator was probably more the norm than most people would like to admit. The reality is that we have been overwhelmed by technology. The changes have been so rapid and so complete that it has become beyond the ability of any individual to understand—we are now dependent on experts to tell us what we need.

Many people tend to see the Internet as overwhelmingly positive. It provides better everything—connectivity, communication, and life experience. To some extent this is true; to be able to talk to and see my best friend and my relatives on Skype or Facebook is a wonderful thing. What is good for the individual does not always extend to the institution. From the standpoint of libraries, the advent of the Internet has meant an endless and seemingly unsolvable series of challenges.

The fundamental problem is that, almost overnight—and for institutions like libraries that measure their existence in centuries, 20 or

30 years is overnight—we have been required to abandon many of our established procedures, customs, and traditions. From what, say in 1980, was a fairly stable system, where librarians understood the procedures and the policies and, moreover, had a reasonable expectation that things would remain as they were, in large part we have moved to a system of constant change, where our techniques, our technology, our very way of working, seemingly changes daily. The list of challenges that face modern libraries could run on almost ad infinitum. The three major ones seem to be: the massive increase in the amount of information, the rapid changes in technology, and, perhaps, the change that people don't often consider, that oftentimes libraries are no longer their own masters.

In the past libraries were, in large part, responsible only to their local constituencies. Sure, there were national standards, such as LC classification or Dewey Decimal, which were established so that libraries had commonalities. That aside, libraries could be, for lack of a better word, individualistic. They could meet the needs of their users as they saw fit in the light of local conditions. To a large extent this was a good thing. Libraries could be more personal. In the modern era libraries are largely shaped and forced into a common mold. The bottom line is that libraries, to a certain extent, no longer have the flexibility to do what they want. They are at the mercy of vendors who make their products for mass consumption. There are common sets of security standards for the Internet. They have to report the same statistics to the federal government.

A most serious problem is that libraries see increasing amounts of their budgets going out to pay for increasingly costly electronic resources and technology—especially electronic journals with associated yearly cost increases. We have moved from the era of fixed costs, where we bought a book once and for all (or at least until it fell apart), to the era of ever-increasing continuing costs, which spans across the entire organization from purchases of materials to new computers to the indirect costs of university overhead to pay for Internet access and sophisticated data centers. Like the university administrator in my earlier example, we are spending larger sums of money on things we don't entirely understand. And, unfortunately, many of these resources, such as electronic serials, often end up underutilized.

How did libraries get in the situation that they are in? In the end I suspect that libraries, like people, end up having lives that reflect the sum of our choices, for good or evil. Personally, and this is perhaps an opinion based more on my experience than on research, it is that we chose not to be more deliberate. When the Internet and the web came along, we could have hung back a little to observe how things developed rather than jumping so quickly into the breach. Being the first (or even the second) adopter of technology is not perhaps the best thing. In hanging back we could have, perhaps, avoided some mistakes. In the case of libraries, perhaps we could have done less or been more deliberate, and ended up in the end with more.

In this book I am going to look at and address these issues in the broadest sense. In my training, in my professional experience, in my life, although I have some understanding and experience with technology, I fully recognize my limitations. My approach to this subject is that of a humanist with some interest in technology rather than as a technologist. My effort is one of trying to give a broad picture of a complex subject with the sincere hope that someone better qualified than I will step in to fill in the gaps I leave or to give rebuttal. My interest in technology is not in technology in and of itself, but in what it can do.

My thought in writing this book is that we can learn from history—perhaps an old-fashioned idea in the era where history is considered irrelevant. The reality, however, is that we have been here before. Other technological innovations, including the telegraph, television, and computers, have been disruptive, but eventually been integrated. In taking a broad humanistic approach, one that considers the history of innovation in the context of libraries, I'm trying to go a step beyond what many books on the Internet do, provide lots of technology terms, lists of quickly outdated websites, and some screen shots. This is an attempt to provide some context for the situation that libraries are in now, so even if, as I say, I end with nothing more than some modest suggestions, at least there will be some perspective and some basis for discussion of the topic, especially for the nontechnically inclined reader.

In some sense this book is something of a hybrid—it is a researched work to be sure. However, I have tried, quite deliberately, to write in a style and manner that will appeal to the general interested person—perhaps an administrator or mid-level manager on a college or university campus. In writing in rather broad strokes, by necessity I have had to leave many things out and not cover some topics in the depth I might have liked, but I hope this book serves as a leaping-off point for the interested reader to find areas of interest and further explore them on their own. My writing style, in some sense, is journalistic and informal. This is by design, and I hope that those who research these topics in depth will recognize my intentions and not judge my modest contribution too harshly. In particular, I suspect my descriptions of networking oversimplify a complicated topic, but I am writing for the interested person and not the technical specialist.

The issue of course in writing any book about the Internet or the World Wide Web or technology is that it rapidly becomes superseded by innovation and events. When I started writing this book, who could have envisioned Arabic revolutions aided and abetted by Twitter? In the time I have been writing this book, technology has advanced dramatically; witness the new dominance of tablet computers, which are rapidly supplanting the laptop, as only one example. Life, it has been said, is what happens when you are making other plans. The same could be said about libraries and the Internet.

CHAPTER 1
Defining the Library

What is a library? In normal usage we can mean it to be anything from a tattered collection of paperbacks by one's bedside to a massive university building holding millions of volumes. Regardless of size one can define a library as a collection of information. These may be books or journals or maps or, in more modern times, electronic databases. Or, more likely, all of these and a hundred other types of things as well.

It would perhaps be more useful to consider a different and broader definition: the library as a technology, a durable consumer good like the telephone system or the telegraph system, that provides a service. But, unlike these earlier technologies, libraries can be repurposed, redesigned, and reengineered for changing times and changing public tastes, which sets them apart from mere technological media, which, inevitably, are superseded and made obsolete by new innovations. Libraries are differentiated by the idea that they have a greater capacity, compared to other technologies, for change and growth. Libraries can be seen as kind of human attempt at artificial evolution that, like biological organisms, competes and evolves within its environment. We deal with the limitations of our own brain size and memory, and, sadly, mortality, by creation of a permanent institution, a library, that stores our information.

The question is, to which this book offers only several modest suggestions, what is the library to become? What are the challenges that the modern evolving library faces? In the course of this discussion we will also try to better define some modern-day terms, such as "Internet," "networking," and such so that readers have a better understanding of what these mean.

THE CURVES OF INNOVATION—MODELS OF CHANGE

Librarians Ross and Pongracz in a 2008 article suggest that people are no longer coming to the library, and indeed various important elements of the library—the online catalog, reference questions, and even librarians themselves—are increasingly outmoded and face a dubious future in the face of competition from such innovations as Google. Ross and Pongracz predict a dark future for libraries, suggesting that they will become increasingly more irrelevant to modern users. They argue that libraries, in spending their resources to support their existing technology infrastructure, leave themselves little or nothing to support future innovation.[1]

The use of an S-curve is one way to understand the development pattern of a technological innovation. As developed by Richard Foster, this curve allows the analysis of the relationship between technological expenditures and the related productivity gains. He sees progress as a situation in which "there may be three or four or more technologies involved in a battle." A more positive and, perhaps, a more useful approach to this issue might be to discuss the future of libraries in terms of a Bass diffusion model. Rather than focus on the issue of rate of adoption of technology versus productivity gains, as does the Foster S-curve, the Bass model is designed for the describing and predicting the purchases of consumer durable products. Librarians and university administrators, obviously, are more interested in the question of whether users are making use of library services than in the issue of comparing the rate of adoption of technology by libraries to society as a whole.[2]

In economic terms libraries could be seen as durable goods since they, both as a class and individually, fit the definition in that they yield a service over time rather than one that is used up in a short while. This allows useful comparison between modern libraries and older consumer technology products such as the Internet, computers, and the telegraph. The Bass model allows libraries to be viewed in terms of users rather than technological innovation (or the lack thereof) within libraries. The future of libraries depends on people using libraries—and technology is only a single factor in determining that outcome.

A diffusion model illustrates innovation spread over time showing the increase in adopters and the penetration of the innovation. In the

Bass model potential adopters have two primary influences: word of mouth and mass media. This makes the Bass model especially useful for libraries since both of these criteria are easily understood and, at least in the case of word of mouth, have always existed. This user-focused approach moves analysis to a broader stage rather than simply creating a technological comparison between libraries—for example, Library A has Technology X; Library B doesn't; Library B is, therefore, somehow a worse library. This is a largely not a useful comparison because libraries differ so vastly in mission, resources, and clients.

If one developed this model, one could see various technological innovations as a sine wave changing over time. Within this, libraries could be viewed as a secondary sine wave whose popularity, or level of adoption among consumers, waxes and wanes partially with the level of technological innovation available within the library. So, for example, in the late 1980s, when libraries had a high level of technological sophistication compared to the world as a whole, they had a peak. With the advent of Google, they entered a valley as Google became seen as more innovative. Public perception drives popularity and use.

Since the mid-1990s, libraries have generally technologically lagged behind the world as a whole, because of lack of funding or other conditions, so these sine waves are not in synch. Prior to that period there wasn't much of a lag since the technology within libraries was stable. Usage may have varied for other reasons, such as rise and fall in user population or differing academic missions that may have focused more or less on the use of libraries—clearly there are some disciplines that make more use of the library than others, despite the best efforts of librarians to convince them otherwise, but technology within the library was not a prime determining factor in patrons deciding whether they would use it. They had few alternatives for information. It may be that libraries will suffer the future that Ross and Pongracz suggest. Seen in terms of the Bass curve, however, individual libraries (and possibly all libraries as a whole, although that remains to be seen) can lag (and probably often do); but if they do innovate, mass media and word of mouth will help make up for their deficits. This suggests that, in an information economy where libraries make effective use of media and treat their users right, they will be successful.

Research on factors causing success in cultural markets seems to confirm this. A 2006 article by Salganik, Dodds, and Watts points out that "social influence contributes to inequality of outcomes in cultural markets, but as individuals are subject to stronger forms of social influence, the collective outcomes will become increasingly unequal."[3] Mass media technologies, such as Google, can be seen as being more effective in creating social influence on users. Libraries have not been as visible or effective in promoting themselves, but they can make up this lag. Libraries may indeed become a different kind of consumer durable good, but they still remain popular in the same way that automobiles have remained popular although steadily changing in technology. Few people today, for example, would want to drive a 1915 Hupmobile as their primary vehicle. That isn't to say they reject automobiles per se. They just want better ones with more features.

Libraries are an evolving consumer durable good that constantly is resold to different generations in different packaging—doing the same job only better. The general theory behind the Bass model asserts that a consumer can adopt a new product only once. The constant shifting of products, books, and databases within a library setting makes libraries always a new product. What does history tell us in regard to the adoption of new technologies and what does this imply for the future of libraries? To understand one revolution it is perhaps useful to start with another.

TECHNOLOGY AND CHANGE

France in 1792 was a society in the midst of extreme change. They were experiencing the ending of the French monarchy, the abolishment of religious congregations, and the removal of the heads of the rulers of the old regime by the new technology of the guillotine. In revolution even the mob eventually reaches their limit of toleration for excess violence and starts looking for other means of expressing their upset. As researcher Ronald Jones noted in a 2005 study on the subject of modern terrorism: "Recognize that beheadings as a tactic have limitations and their popularity will wane as security conditions improve, since the tactic is dependent on unstable conditions." Such was the case in 1793, in a society seeking stability from revolution, when Frenchman M. Claude Chappe's first two attempts to construct a telegraph between Paris and Lille were destroyed by the population, in the second instance by burning his station completely to the ground, who wrongly suspected he was communicating with royalist prisoners. Still violence to be sure, but directed more at property than persons—which any reasonable person should see as some kind of improvement. Chappe's subsequent later efforts, now under the aegis of the new French government, an optical system based on the use of signal flags raised in combination, were more successful as they represented an attempt at progress and order under the new regime. In the territorial expansion that characterized Napoleonic France, the advantages of such a communications system found a ready audience among French officials. His telegraph system was adopted in Denmark (1802), England (1795), and elsewhere, and was used in France until the 1850s when it was finally supplanted by the electric telegraph. The work of M. Chappe and subsequent communication innovations represented a long-standing desire by mankind for quick two-way information exchange. From ancient times communication has often been, slow and uncertain, subject to the caprices of weather, road and sea conditions, and misadventure.[4]

The use of fire for communication is found in some of the earliest texts. The Bible says in the book of Jeremiah (1:6), "Flee for safety, ye children of Benjamin, out of the midst of Jerusalem, and blow the trumpet in Tekoa, and raise up a signal on Beth-haccherem; for evil looketh forth from the north, and a great destruction." Mention of the use of fire signaling, mostly in a military context, can be found in a variety of later ancient writers such as the Roman historian Polybius.[5]

It became relatively easy to send simple messages of the "yes/no" variety quickly. Paul Revere could easily see the signal "one if by land, two if by sea" sent by the lanterns in the tower of the Old North Church. To get this message into the countryside he had to borrow Deacon Larkin's horse and ride. Communication of more complex information through development of a regular technological network of fast two-way communications had to await the growth of better technology and organized governmental and business infrastructures stable and robust enough to provide the support—financial, legal, and technological—needed for widespread successful implementation. This change awaited development of a perceived need among the general public that such a system was desirable and necessary. In France the conservative counterreaction of the Napoleonic era to the excesses of the Terror led to what historian Howard Brown, referring to Michel Foucault's idea of "governmentality," conceives as a "security state" based in part on government use of technology for repression of dissent—so the reaction of the locals to M. Chappe's innovation becomes somewhat understandable. Modernity is suspect.[6]

Upset about new technology seems to be a central component of modernity. A 1941 article by science editor Waldemar Kaempffert at the *New York Times* makes the point that people operate in a system and tend to create their worldview within the confines of that system. It was not simply an issue of introducing a new technology that mattered so much as the act itself requires people to revise and reexamine a whole system of attitudes and practice, which, quite frankly, people left on their own would not do. The result was a technological lag as society struggled to choke down new innovations. War was a unique situation in that it accelerated and forced these changes:

Both in industry and war men are regulated. Everywhere there is system—system in reconnoitering from the air, firing shells from a battery, building an airplane, preparing and packing breakfast food. Innovations can be introduced in the midst of war on a small and experimental scale, as in the case of gas, the tank, and armored vessels.[7]

Societies make great psychological and capital investment in the existing state of affairs—social and technological—and, with few exceptions, one rarely sees a society engaging in a rapid wholesale change in anything except when the change is so revolutionary (automobiles, electricity) that not changing would be disastrous. Change in human history, considered on the whole, is a gradual thing. This, in some sense, is what makes the development of the Internet so remarkable an event. Like the telephone system or the telegraph before it, it has transformed in a very short amount of time the entire way society conducts its affairs although perhaps not without some doubters in the crowd.

This ambiguity about the value of technological innovation can be seen in the example of expansion of railway service to Oxford University. This was seen by university faculty as a detriment to the scholarship and morals of students. The university took care to ensure it wasn't negatively impacted, having Parliament include language in the 1843 enabling act stating:

If the said Vice-Chancellor [etc.] shall . . . notify to the proper Officers, Book-keeper, or Servant of said Company that any Person or Persons about to travel in or upon said Railway is a Member of the University not having taken the Degree of Master of Arts or Bachelor in Civil Law, and require such Officer . . . to decline to take such Member of the University thereupon, and for the space of 24 hours . . . refuse to covet Such member of the said University.[8]

Like the railway the telegraph was suspect to the English. It was new. It was innovative. It was French.

One sees similar tendencies in popular culture. European artistic traditions in the early nineteenth century favored depictions of historic scenes designed to impart moral virtue, such as Delacroix's "Liberty Leading the People" or William Payne's pastoral scenes of rural England. Depictions of modern life, of the inventions such as the trains and factories, transforming society or simply people in their everyday lives were noticeably absent. It is only in the latter decades of the nineteenth century that we see the emergence of new disciplines of sociology, psychology, and artistic modes, such as Impressionism, that, like the novels of Émile Zola, challenged romantic idealism with realistic depictions of modern life. In the mid-nineteenth century occurs convergence of those disparate elements, such as financial capital, technological innovation, and an emerging public sentiment favoring progress, needed to create an international telegraph system—in some sense the ancestor of our modern Internet. The telegraph was itself the outgrowth of an earlier technological interest—electricity.

ELECTRICAL MANIA

Since ancient times philosophers have asked: What energy made a man lives? And then stop? And where did it go? It was only in the sixteenth century that this concept gained the name "electricity." William Gilbert, the doctor to Queen Elizabeth I and an early scientist, coined the term while investigating the phenomenon, which at the time was thought of as some kind of universal "ether" permeating the world. In the eighteenth century discoveries by Italians Galvani Luigi and Alessandro Volta led to the invention of the battery, making research into electricity move rapidly from simple and popular public demonstrations of electrostatics to practical applications.[9]

THE PRACTICAL DEVELOPMENT OF THE TELEGRAPH

It was only a short time until people turned their minds to the idea of using electricity for practical communication, although the beginnings of the idea had been suggested much earlier. The Italian Jesuit Strada, for example, had written in 1617 about using separated pieces of lodestone attached to dials with letters for communication, where moving one magnetic needle would move the other regardless of the distance between the two. The eighteenth century was the time when theory became practical application. In July 1747 Dr. Watson, Bishop of Llandaff, passed electricity through the waters of the Thames. From the 1780s onward there were various attempts at developing electric telegraphs, for example, with combinations of needles or pins that would vibrate upon application of current and point to letters and numbers on a board. By the 1840s such systems had been superseded by that of Samuel Morse, which depended on sending patterns of electric clicks.[10]

NETWORKS AND NERVES

In trying to understand the modern Internet, it is important to realize that, despite the differences in technology, the fundamental idea of networking is the same. From 1800 onward the idea of a standing network of connections between places (and individuals) gained increasing acceptance, largely though public recognition of the usefulness of such networks in meeting public goals. The telegraph served as a tool to transform individual perception of time and space, in enabling creation of universal standards of measurement, such as the development of Greenwich Mean Time as a national (and eventually world) time standard, and in furthering transnational political and economic systems.

Historian Iwan Morus refers to the desire for "instantaneous knowledge" feeding into the Victorian desire for order and discipline, for which the telegraph was an admirably suited tool. The network of telegraph wires was seen as a metaphor for the nerves of the human body, serving the same purpose in helping the mind regulate the body's actions. This is an interesting contrast to the role of the modern Internet, which is seen, in many instances, less as an instrument of regulation than a tool that allows individuals to escape (or defy) the power of the state—the advent of blogging and social networking sites, such as Facebook, being prime examples. There are clearly useful parallels between the modern Internet and earlier technologies, but this also serves to remind us that we need to always view the past in terms of the values of the times. To simply see the Victorians as top-hatted versions of ourselves, with the same moral and social values, is to engage in a most inaccurate kind of historical revisionism. In very important ways they were quite different, especially in that they were really quite less individualistic in their attitudes and behaviors. To them what society thought did matter.[11]

The growing telegraph network, although it served private business and personal needs, also met a public purpose by increasing the ability of the state to provide services and social welfare, as is seen in the case of John Byron. In 1848 he was convicted of forgery, having stolen some loose checks and forged the owner's signature in a case that echoes the modern problem of identity theft. He was captured at Newcastle-upon-Tyne by use of the "electronic telegraph." The telegraph also was used for solving more serious crimes. In 1845 chemist and druggist John Tawell murdered his former servant, Sarah Hart, with whom he had been having a romantic affair, by poisoning her with prussic acid, discussion of which formed a large part of the trial, illustrating something about the emerging role of forensic science in the criminal justice system. In January 1845 he was captured, in large part because London police were telegraphed from where he had taken the train at Slough, allowing the police to meet the train at London's Paddington Station and, following him, find evidence of his guilt, resulting in his trial and subsequent execution in March 1845. Ironically, in 1814 he had not been hung for counterfeiting, which shows how one can delay one's appointment in Samarra but never avoid it altogether.[12]

THE INTERNATIONALIZATION OF NETWORKS

The use of the telegraph became an essential element for national governments in managing their affairs within a relatively short period of time. The British Empire made great use of the telegraph to maintain a worldwide administrative structure. There was, after the 1850s, establishment of an international network of telegraph cables, both land based and submarine, financed by a combination of government and private monies. Britain had a dominant role in the development of this international telecommunications structure because it had, like the United States in the development of the Internet during the 1980s and 1990s, the economic capital, technical infrastructure, and political will to develop the system.

In the development of both landline and submarine cable systems British companies and, later, the British government took a leading role. Cable communications became a central element of imperial strategy after 1870, especially in relation to communications with central parts of the Empire, such as India, with the development of the idea of an "all-red" system that didn't cross foreign soil at any point and was thus immune to tampering. By 1892 Britain had 163,618 km of cables, compared to 38,987 km by the United States—which clearly reflects the imperial ambitions of Britain, as opposed to the United States, which was focused on the taming of its own wild interior.

This development of an international communications system led to the creation of a system of treaties and international organizations to administer and standardize the newly emerging technology with the aim toward the development of a kind of nascent economic globalization. Economist Armand Mattelart in his book *Networking the World, 1794–2000* observes:

The deployment of technological networks during the second half of the nineteenth century perpetuated the worldwide economic integration initiated at the turn of the seventeenth century with the expansion of the Dutch East India Company in 1602 and its monopoly of the spice trade. In a world that still seemed to offer limitless possibilities for exploration and exploitation, networks played their part in the new parceling out of the planet that redefined the parameters of national economies.[13]

It is possible to see in the development of this new communication system many of the problems that beset the creation of the Internet later: cooperation (and conflict) between private groups and government agencies, the need for development of accepted standards, and changing public attitudes toward technology, all accomplished in an atmosphere of rapid technological and social change.

One can see how the creation of communication networks went hand in hand with an overwhelming interest in the theory and practice of science. The nineteenth century, a century of technological innovation, including the development of cheap, readily available books printed on wood pulp as opposed to the earlier more expensive linen, was also a century of increased general public interest in science. Popular publication of science books, both groundbreaking intellectual works such as Charles Darwin's *Origin of Species* (1859) as well as inexpensive yet high-quality illustrated popularizations describing natural phenomena (animals, plants, and insects), reached much wider audiences. In this environment the idea and practice of networks became widely accepted. The telegraph network was quickly paralleled (and later replaced) by the telephone system and, later, radio. In these developments can be seen recognition of the need for ever-increasing bandwidth to support increasingly complicated forms of communication.[14]

THE TWENTIETH-CENTURY NETWORK: CHANGES IN PERCEPTION OF DISTANCE AND TIME

One of the most famous Americans in 1937 was Howard Hughes—not as the crazed recluse he later became, holed up in the Desert Inn of 1960s Las Vegas watching endless reruns of *Ice Station Zebra*, but as a world-famous aviator who routinely set records for speed and distance in a series of innovative aircraft. His popularity was attributable, at least in part to the idea that Americans of the early and mid-twentieth century were obsessed with the idea of conquering space and time, obsessed by the idea of being able to go faster from A to Z. In the exploits of Hughes and other famous aviators, in the development of streamlined passenger trains able to go from New York to Los Angeles in four days, and in new and improved highway systems, one sees similar themes—a fascination with technology and the idea of progress.[15]

Communication networks were part of these trends. More house-holds had access to telephones, and with the wide availability of cheap radios and the development of national radio networks one sees the glimmerings of a modern mass media culture. Broadcast entertainment and the effective use of the media by politicians show the beginning of the creation of a sense of national identity on the basis of identification with popular culture on a larger and more invasive scale. This develop-ing mass media, while being without the two-way interactivity of the modern Internet, did create a sense of connectedness that made people begin to look beyond their own community and region to seeing them-selves as members of a more global community. Changes in the labor market from an agricultural to an industrial economy gave individuals the economic means and free time to indulge in leisure that included mass media, such as the newsreel routinely shown before nearly all movies. From around 1930 onward there was also the beginning of tele-vision, notably the German broadcast of the 1936 Olympic Games, and, in England, even crude attempts at home video recording of televi-sion broadcasts. In 1930s Germany, Hitler used technology, radio, film, and television in a limited way as propaganda tools.[16]

There was in some quarters a sense of foreboding about technological innovations. Like contemporary critics of the Internet, such as com-puter scientist and author Clifford Stoll who wrote in 1995 about his concerns of the negative effects of the Internet on libraries and informa-tion, there was earlier worry about the effect of the new mass culture and the technological innovations accompanying it, as the increasing speed of life threatened traditional values and ways of doing things, especially in the development of what might be called a "culture of interruption" where people no longer had time for quiet study. In a 1923 speech at Brown University, Secretary of State Charles Evans Hughes observed that "it was the day of the fleeting vision. Concentration, thoroughness, the quiet reflection that ripens judgment are more difficult than ever."[17]

As with the Oxford faculty and their concerns about trains in the 1840s, there was a feeling by some that the new technologies would negatively impact public morals. Radio networks, despite their positive benefit in exposing people to religion, also had the potential to cut church attendance. A radio listener could simply flip a switch or turn a dial whereas the "disgruntled hearer had to face the moral disapproval of the congregation and his own sense of shame if he leaves before time." Concern about moral issues went hand in hand with technological innovation. In the mass media, film scandals such as the Fatty Arbuckle murder trial led to a conservative backlash of self-censorship through use of a motion picture production code administered by puritanical former postmaster general Will Hays. This parallels developments with the Internet where, in absence of applicable laws, which lagged technological progress, and amid similar concerns about the effects on public morals, the marketplace acted, through the development of filtering devices and internal processes such as rating systems for video games, to address societal concerns about content.[18]

The fundamental underlying issue was the growth in the amount of information available to the public. As the mass media culture began to come of age, existing societal mechanisms for controlling and regulating information began to break down. The faster pace in the amount of knowledge created, coupled with faster delivery mechanisms, meant that individuals had increasing difficulty in sorting and organizing information. This led to recognition of the need for better tools for knowledge management, which ultimately led to the development of modern computing and the Internet.

THE INTRODUCTION OF THE COMPUTER

From the mid-nineteenth century, there had been various kinds of mechanical calculators available. The growing need for various kinds of mathematical tables, for engineering, architecture, and finance, led to the development of commonly used books, often called ready reckoners, containing useful tables and formulas. In everyday life if one looked for the definition of "computers," it would be, literally, a roomful of people called "computers" who worked with primitive manual adding devices (or pencil and paper) doing hand calculations. This profession, now gone the way of the lamplighter, came into being in the early nineteenth century. The earliest computers, oddly enough, were French hairdressers put out of work by the French Revolution. They presumably had both attention to detail and the willingness to do tedious work.[19] The inevitable mistakes that crept into such books through human error led to a variety of attempts to produce better mechanical calculators.[20]

Among the earliest and most famous of these attempts were those developed by Englishman Charles Babbage, often acknowledged as the originator of the idea of computing as we now understand it. Babbage formalized many of the basic principles later used in electronic computers including input-output devices, programming, and central storage of information. Although his machines were never actually constructed, largely for lack of money, a working replica of one of Babbage's earlier designs was constructed in the 1990s using nineteenth-century techniques and materials, proving the soundness of his conception.[21]

The work of Babbage later influenced many fiction writers leading to the formation beginning in the 1970s of an entire literary genre, "steampunk," which often used Babbage's computers as a plot element. Bruce Sterling and William Gibson's 1990 novel *The Difference Engine* postulated a future in which Babbage's machines were actually built in the 1850s, introducing the computer age a century earlier than it actually happened. This influence inspires developers of the modern Internet (the online world Second Life, for example, has an entire area devoted to steampunk), showing how technological innovations influence popular culture and spark future development.[22]

Growing recognition of the need for better and larger systems for storing and retrieving information to keep up with the increasing production of knowledge was not, in the early twentieth century, matched by technological progress. The computers that existed, although more complex than earlier machines, were little better in terms of function than those available in Charles Babbage's day, mostly used for very simple but repetitive kinds of calculations, like adding up census data or figuring out the tables needed to accurately compute proper trajectories for artillery shells. One especially utilitarian example was a mechanical tide predictor, which used a set of wheels and gears to do the tedious and time-consuming work of adding various wave heights. Computers were, quite literally, large mechanical devices full of gears and metal rods that, to be useful, had to be disassembled and set up for each problem—a process that could take days. It was strictly a hardware-based solution—both expensive and cumbersome. Often human calculators, cheaper and faster than machines, were still preferred.[23]

THE CODE BREAKERS AND THE BOMB MAKERS

We must first ask a question before we continue: what is a computer? In daily life this is a straightforward question that most people know the answer to: a small electronic box that does X, Y, or Z. Computers come in all shapes and sizes—a cell phone is a kind of computer as is a massive supercomputer. There are computers in cars and appliances. We generally think of those lovely plastic boxes with which we have a love/hate relationship in our homes and offices.

One could presumably, given proper and sufficiently complex arrangements, produce a machine that could emulate any other machine, even a human brain. One can see rather quickly that this raises numerous complicated questions about the nature of human consciousness, free will, and other philosophical issues. Is there (or could there potentially be) a mind embodied in a computer conscious in the sense we normally understand human consciousness? Would such a device be a computer—a technological device or a new form of intelligent life? This is a question well beyond our scope, but it makes clear that underlying our daily experience with the common desktop computer are serious intellectual and philosophical issues worth considering. The more important question, from the standpoint of libraries what is the effect when the ubiquity and level of sophistication of computers becomes such that the role of libraries as a storage location for information becomes moot? If information becomes embedded in our daily environment do we need libraries as physical places? Is there some point where the library no longer serves as a material repository of objects and, instead, becomes solely a location used for network access and a facilitator for intellectual collaboration for people separated physically by thousands of miles?

Returning from philosophy to history, we can see in code breaking that the idea of machines emulating machines, suggested above, comes truly into its own. The British government established a large code-breaking establishment at Bletchley Park in Buckinghamshire where, ultimately, 7,000 people worked at decoding German messages. In large part they were able to do this through a combination of brainpower—employing many of the most intelligent people in the country from mathematics professors to chess masters and using primitive computers, called "bombes" because of the ticking noise they made while running, that went through every possible permutation of letters in a message to decode it. The British were trying to catch up with the Germans. The German government, secretly rearming in defiance of the Treaty of Versailles after World War I, found quick utility in commercially available cryptography devices for communication. With the outbreak of World War II, the need to break these German codes, previously not a high priority, became urgent. The war forced the rapid development of faster and better mechanical (and, later, electronic) computers thus demonstrating the point made by Waldemar Kaempffert.[24]

Weapons design was the other area where computers were used during the war. Atomic bombs are math writ large. To understand an atomic explosion one must be able to comprehend all the events that are happening within the first milliseconds of the reaction. This is a decidedly nontrivial task, in terms of both the amount of data and the repetition of the needed calculations—so much so that it makes designing and building atomic weapons expensive and difficult, explaining why since 1945 (and one hopes for some time to come) few countries have had the resources to successfully construct them. From 1942 onward, with the development of the first primitive electronic computers these machines took an increasingly important role as it was realized that these devices, even in their primitive form which required the use of punched cards, originally designed for specific purposes such as breaking codes or calculating the orbits of planets, could be used in more generalized ways such as doing actual war simulations.[25]

ISLANDS OF INFORMATION

Computers were seen in the 1950s, in large part, as simply a form of electronic data storage. For some obvious purposes, like the federal census, there was recognition that basic numerical calculations would need to be accomplished, but that was about it. The idea of a personal computer that one would use in daily life for productivity purposes or communication was as alien as the dark side of the moon. Computers were large, expensive, and, it was assumed, would stay that way. This had been largely the perception in the public mind, through the limited use of calculating machinery by governments since the late nineteenth century, largely for census and statistical purposes, and even the technological changes of World War II were slow in making their way into wide practice. Any nineteenth-century librarian entering a library of the 1940s and 1950s would have stood within its walls and understood his or her environment almost immediately and felt at home. For the most part libraries did their operations without really changing their organization and practices. Computers were not something that librarians saw much need for. It is only in the 1960s that computers began to be used for bulk database operations such as the production of catalog cards. It is only from the late 1970s and early 1980s that there was recognition by librarians that computers had some usefulness outside of technical services to improve traditional public services activities, such as replacing the venerable card catalog, a transformational event in the history of libraries. The developers of online catalogs didn't even see them as something that individual libraries would have and would be transformational within individual institutions. Instead, they would join consortiums and develop a common catalog, accessible to all. In 1980, as one example, the New England Library Network (NELINET) announced the development of online catalogs on a time-share basis. The primary focus wasn't even on developing electronic catalogs, but instead "to promote or develop the means for a variety of computer-based systems to 'talk' to each other." Over time NELINET, like many other regional organizations, developed so that today it serves as a regional consortial purchasing agent for databases and training partner with New England libraries, providing no telecommunications or time-share computing services at all. It is the shift to the Internet which changed everything and, perhaps, for that, a brief nontechnical description of how networking works would be useful.[26]

THE INTERNET: AN EXPLANATION FOR THE NONTECHNICALLY INCLINED

To understand how the Internet works one must understand that the transmission of data is inherently "bursty." We see this in everyday life. Say at a cocktail party, where, in one corner, you have a bore going on for 30 minutes about pig belly futures. That's how a typical telephone conversation works; the circuit remains open and occupied whether or not anything is being said. A data transmission is more like two people, at the same party, who have short intense conversations punctuated by silence. "What do you think the meaning of life is?"—then silence, followed by a long, intense answer. And, two feet away, two other people standing next to them have their own conversation, similarly punctuated by silences. There are multiple conversations going on in the same room, conversations that are mostly empty space, but they don't interfere with each other.

The Internet, put simply, is a technical system designed to take this idea of "burstyness" and use it most effectively, allowing multiple conversations to be sent over the same line at the same time. Each piece of information is divided into individual portions, called packets, that can then be sent along intermixed, in much the same way that a conveyer belt at Federal Express moves packages. The system cares that the packages are a uniform size, but it's irrelevant whether one box has auto parts and the next clothing, just that they are properly packaged and labeled so the system can direct them automatically to the proper delivery truck. The technology for the Internet that does this is complicated and, alas for administrators, expensive, but the fundamental idea is the same.

The other idea essential to understanding the Internet is the idea of networking. The Internet uses computers to digitally connect different computers (and different people) through the creation of a standard system of addresses and connections. If I work at, say, Possum University and have a Possum University e-mail address in English, librarianguy@ possum.edu, the Internet, through a series of technical steps, rules, and database tables, translates these words into a technical address so that, when my friend at Raccoon University, librariangirl@Raccoon.edu, sends me an e-mail the message is properly routed by the system so it ends up in my e-mail box and no one else's. You may wonder how this works.

Once Upon a Time . . .

there was a town called Circleville—quite properly because every building in the town was arranged facing a ring road that went completely in a circle. Circleville was unusual in that none of the inhabitants ever wanted to go outside.

So to communicate they hired a postman, Mr. Boring. Now, Mr. Boring was just that. Boring. He did nothing but walk around this circle picking up and delivering letters—24 hours a day, seven days a week. At every house he did things exactly the same way. He picked up the letters left in the mailbox and dropped off the ones that needed to be delivered. And he did this in exactly the same order, opening the mailbox with his right hand, putting his left hand in his mailbag and pulling out the letters, which he then put in the mailbox, which he then closed, always with his right hand. And then, putting his left foot out first, he started to the next house.

We should mention that, in order to make Mr. Boring's life easier, each envelope had messages of exactly the same length—with an address written at both ends, so if you wanted to write a long message, you had to send two messages like:

Header-Address

IxlovexRita

Footer—Address End of message

Header-Address

Shexlovsxme

Footer—Address—End of message

So even though each message has only 11 characters, one could, by sending multiple messages, send a message as long as necessary. Mr. Boring's great skill was that he could effortlessly keep all the messages sorted in his head as to where they were in his bag. So with the message above, sent by Mr. B to his wife, Mrs. B, who was at work in the building down the way, Mr. Boring could, when he got to Mrs. B's workplace, without effort or looking pull those two messages above out of his bag, from among hundreds of similar envelopes, and put them in Mrs. B's mailbox, where her assistant could sort them, put them in the right order, and put them on Mrs. B's desktop.

Now, every house was arranged differently on the interior, and so some people wanted their mail on the desktop in the library and some wanted it delivered to the morning room, but as long they followed the same rules and had a mailbox of a uniform size and shape, they could still get their mail. Mr. Boring didn't especially care what happened to the letters inside the house, as long as each house followed the rules about length and format of the letters and he could follow his rules for delivering them.

What happened when, say, Mr. B needed to send a letter to his friend, Mr. C, who lived in Starville several miles away? And keep in mind, Starville, unlike Circleville, was arranged like a star. There was a central hub with each house having its own separate street. The mailman in Starville, unlike Mr. Boring, walked from the post office to a house, back to the post office, got another letter, and walked to the next house. But he followed the same rules: open the mailbox with the right hand, put the mail in with the left hand, close the box with the right hand, start off on the left foot to the next house. (We should mention that, to keep things honest, every mailman was followed by a monitor. If he saw that the mail was being dropped or not delivered, he could yell out and the process would start over again from the beginning.)

At a certain place on the ring Mr. Boring had a colleague, Mr. K, to whom he gave all the messages that were going away from Circleville. Mr. K's job (and great talent) was the ability to know how to get messages to other places the fastest way. At any given moment he knew about the traffic everywhere—where there were delays, where the road was clear—so he could quickly hand out the letters to one of a series of dispatch riders (along with instructions on the quickest way to get there), who would then speed off on a motorcycle to deliver the message.

* * *

What we've described here is basically how the Internet works. You have people working on one network (Circleville) who put their messages into a preformatted standardized format of a uniform length (a packet) where they are picked up from their mailbox (their computer) by a person working in a certain way (standardized Internet protocols). When a message needs to go a long distance, it is handed over to a specialist, Mr. K (in Internet terms a specialized piece of software called a router), who determines the best way to send the message and puts it on its way through the Internet to its intended destination. Included in the system is programming that translates the human e-mail address librarianguy@possum.edu or whatever into a numerical code, and likewise for the person to whom the e-mail is addressed, so the message goes to that one person it is intended for and none other. One can see that the Internet lets people on different kinds of networks, arranged in different ways (or topologies), communicate because, even though they are arranged differently, they follow the same underlying rules. The Internet also doesn't especially care what kind of house (computer/ operating system) you have as long as it follows the same underlying rules (protocols), which include a system of fault detection (the monitor) to tell the users if the system fails.[27]

THE CREATION OF THE MODERN INTERNET

The origin of the idea of the Internet is often attributed to engineer and public policy expert Vannevar Bush, but this is incorrect. Most of his work that dealt with computing was concerned with analog mechanical computers. His 1945 *Atlantic Monthly* article "As We May Think" is seen as introducing the idea of the Internet, and, indeed, he is seen perhaps as being the spiritual father of the Internet. While it is true that Bush recognized the importance of the relationship of rapid exchange of information and the development of the modern technological state, it is probably overstating the case to see him as the proto-innovator of our modern Internet. His conception was not so much a digital computer that could run a corporation as creating a device which would enhance civilization by giving people full access to the information (and associations between those data) that they collected in their daily lives.[28]

When his ideas are examined closely, it can be seen that his primary interest was information retrieval (especially as it relates to microfilm) rather than the development of computer networks. Bush actually saw computers as being impractical from an engineering standpoint and certainly not something that individuals would own as individual appliances. Philosophically, if one considers his views on the relationship of science and government, it also appears quite clear that the uncontrolled Internet of today was the furthest thing from his mind and, indeed, being a staunch social and political conservative, he would probably be both appalled and offended by both the content of the present Internet and the quasi-chaos in which it operates. If anything, Bush was somewhat statist in his approach—in some ways reflecting the technological fixations of the 1930s—seeing the role of scientists and engineers as working hand in glove, often with government, to organize progress in a very structured manner.

THE DEVELOPMENT OF THE DATABASE

The real problem that Bush and others faced in the 1940s was that of organizing large bodies of data and relating them to each other. A key element in the development of the modern Internet as a useful information tool is the idea of the relational database. Up until the 1960s most computerized information was simply counted. The kind of computations that, say, the Census Bureau needed done, knowing how many people lived in a particular place, were easy to do. What was more difficult was seeing how different data sets related to one another. What was the relationship between race and poverty? How could the data be used to forecast future trends and better society? Being able to access the information in the database required knowing its physical structure.

Keep in mind that much of the computing in the 1950s and 1960s was not real-time data analysis. Users simply entered their data on punch cards, which were fed through a card reader; the data were collected; and they were analyzed according to some predetermined program. If someone, for example, decided that they actually wanted to do some different analysis, they had to set up the computer again, submit a second set of cards, and redo the process. The kind of rapid "what-if" modeling that one can commonly see in modern computers and software simply didn't exist. Computing was slow, expensive, and centralized—usually in some single remote computer room where normal users were not admitted.

One simple way to understand this is to look at a basic spreadsheet. Most people have used some form of spreadsheet, such as Microsoft Excel, at some time or another. Spreadsheets were originally developed in the late 1970s for financial applications, although earlier versions of this software had existed in the mid-1960s. With the development of the personal computer and its use in business environments, the spreadsheet as a tool really took off, with VisiCalc, Lotus-1-2-3, and Microsoft Excel all being widely accepted in the marketplace. This was largely because, for the first time, it gave average computer users the ability to do their own limited form of computer modeling, and the ability to add different variables and explore different scenarios on their own in more or less real time. This is a vast philosophical difference between the way computing had been done previously. True, the kinds and types of analysis that could be performed were limited, but it was a serious paradigm shift in the decentralization of data analysis, something that echoes to this day in how individuals and parts of organizations organize and manipulate their information resources.

Now, although spreadsheets work very well for seeing small amounts of data and for doing a limited amount of analysis, say adding up expenses where you can see the various data elements, they rapidly become much too large (and slow) to be practical to use. What sensible person would try to drill through a grid of 10,000 by 10,000 elements trying to find information? And this gets even more complicated when trying to look at different spreadsheets and see the relationship between data in each.

A relational database, on the other hand, unhooks the physical storage, the arrangement of the data from the logical organization. From about 1970 onward, this development of a relational system became more and more the standard way to present and analyze data, beginning with the seminal work of researcher Edgar F. Codd who was one of first people to seriously develop the concept. Along the way there was the development of a number of different query languages—Ingres, System R, and, eventually, Structured Query Language (SQL), which became the accepted standard for doing database queries. Coupled with the explosive development of the Internet this gave rise to sophisticated online database systems, accessible through web interfaces, which makes both e-commerce and the modern online library catalog possible.[29]

HOW A RELATIONAL DATABASE WORKS

A relational database works because different tables in a database share a common field. For example, if you have a library catalog database, you might have one table with all the fields relating to purchasing information, another table with all the detailed cataloging information, and a third table with just the information the user needs to find the book, e.g., call number and physical location. Each of these tables is linked by some specific common piece of information such as the title—call it a common key. By doing a search that contains this common field, you are able to create a result that combines the separate information in each table.

For example, let's say that in Table 1 we have the fields of the common key and price, in Table 2 we have the common key and bibliographic information including publication date, and in Table 3 we have the common key and the circulation history of the item. Using the accepted Structured Query Language (SQL), we can create a question for the database—e.g., Show me all the books costing over $50 published by Harper and Row that have circulated only three times or less. One can see that, as a budget management tool, this is very useful, especially if you use the report function, commonly available in most database products, to create regular reports on what you are spending and where. The use of various programming languages, coupled with the Internet, allows the database producer to create a different look and feel for the various kinds of users that they expect. A library catalog for example will look very different from the web page for Amazon.com. Underneath they share some striking similarities in their basic architecture, although, in the case of Amazon, there are undoubtedly specialized (and proprietary) aspects to their programming that give them advantages in their business, especially in terms of tracking the buying habits of users.[30]

The use of this "common key" lets users create an almost infinite set of relationships between the data in the various tables. Of course, in normal practice with modern online catalogs, you never actually put in a "raw" database query but instead use a series of predefined search boxes to search through the database. The confusion for users (and the cost for administrators) is that there is a wide range of online catalogs (and database products) that, although they share the same "under the hood" functionality, look vastly different and operate differently. The traditional library card catalog, on the other hand, looked the same regardless of what library you went into. This has been a criticism of the development of library online catalogs by writers such as Nicholson Baker, who in a seminal 1996 article on libraries lamented the loss of this common cultural experience.[31]

To some extent these critics have a point, but they ignore the fact that the paper system simply wasn't a sustainable model in terms of either production or maintenance, or simply from the standpoint of physical space in the library. The online catalog offers opportunities and advantages to libraries that result in both better intellectual access and lowered administrative costs. And, in the end, proponents of the paper catalog ignore the fact that most users simply don't care. They just want their book and favor any system that gets them that book faster. This is, essentially, the core problem facing modern libraries. There is a constant demand for increased services for users at the same time there are flat or reduced resource bases. Libraries are forced to change with the times. Their challenge is how to take their users along with them on the trip.

THE MESSY FUTURE FOR UNIVERSITY LIBRARIES

This should be prefaced by the comment that we are discussing university and college libraries. Public and corporate libraries operate quite differently, for different clienteles, and with quite different funding models. While the comments here may apply to those kinds of libraries, it should be observed that there are limits in how far one can extend these comments to those kinds of organizations. University libraries are often progressive units. They understand technology and the information needs of their users. Yet they often operate within conservative organizations. Higher education generally embraces evolutionary not revolutionary change. In addition, the nature of the organizational structure and funding models, and especially in public universities the need for accountability to bodies such as boards of regents or state legislatures, means that academic libraries don't always have lots of flexibility in how they approach their mission. The university, and the library by extension, is increasingly dominated by a business model that often places cost containment at a higher priority than scholarly mission. Innovation is recognized as important, but libraries are not always structured, or, unfortunately, supported by their administrations, in ways that make accomplishing that mission easy.

The central role of academic libraries, regardless of issues providing access or facilitating intellectual growth often largely remains that of an archive. That isn't to say that librarians don't do that in newer and more complex ways with better technology than their predecessors, but in the end libraries generally don't create information as their primary purpose. They harvest it selectively from the totality of knowledge, organize it, and store it, in the hope that someone at some time will need it. It is true that modern libraries provide a wide array of new services, including access to computers and wireless networks or social amenities such as cafés. Libraries have also, to lesser or greater degrees, been reasonably good in lessening barriers to users, such as eliminating library fines and creating usable online catalogs, but basic structural conservatism often remains. This is a missed opportunity for libraries: the creation of new sources of information and the development of collaboration with users throughout the institution and the community seems the key to making the library viable in the future.

That aside, philosophically, many librarians in higher education seem to be idealistic technocrats working from a romanticized tradition idealizing the idea of the continuity of knowledge and learning along with the traditions and practices of academe. Libraries have traditionally been seen as closed sets of knowledge capable of being organized and managed in some meaningful sense. The very idea of a cataloging department, for example, implies that information can somehow be arranged into particular areas, when the reality is that borders between disciplines are rapidly fading. There is rigorous interest in modeling academic faculty achievements and standards for research and professional activity—along with their various academic titles, such as assistant professor, or associate professor—regardless of whether or not, in practice, their activities actually truly mirror the roles of academic faculty. This, in some cases, perhaps does a disservice to librarians—at least in terms of the public perception of their roles. Providing direct public service, as opposed to that of the pure academic research scholar, is an important one that should not be marginalized or discounted as libraries benefit from being multifaceted in their approaches to service. As a 2010 article on library organization points out:

Also like universities, libraries are characterized by multiple, often quite distinct, subcultures. It is therefore likely that a given library's profile would contain a mix of two or more dominant cultural types. This challenges leadership to manage and, where desirable, cultivate distinct and potentially competing cultures within the library organization.[32]

Librarians, at least in the United States, also come from the intellectual tradition of the Enlightenment that sees progress being the result of planning. Librarians want a managed future: libraries that are the result of careful planning, data analysis, and consultation with experts. Libraries are seen as places that will meet the needs of users in a comprehensive way by the use of carefully administered plans, ideologically pure, scientifically sound, and politically neutral, that will bring order to informational chaos.

Librarians are trying to operate in a world where long-term planning for knowledge collection makes less and less sense. In an Internet-dominated world, information is not only decentralized and expanding, but also becoming obsolete. A hundred years ago a librarian could buy a history book on ancient Rome knowing, based on experience, there was a reasonable expectation that people would always be interested in the subject. The reality now is that whole areas of knowledge can simply expire and go dark for lack of interest. There is no longer that long-term expectation for the worth of all particular areas of knowledge. Yet librarians still plan for the future in the context of an archival model, moving the "dark" knowledge to remoter and remoter storage facilities—physical facilities farther and farther from the main campus or electronic databases of increasing size ad infinitum. This passive archival approach to knowledge is outdated. What is required are bold efforts to develop innovative ways to engage students and faculty in being creative learners and partners with the library. Examples could be a writing instruction collaboration between library and instructional faculty as George Washington University has done since 2004 or service learning opportunities as has been implemented at Wright State University.[33]

Progress often comes from trial and error and from making mistakes not from grand central planning. The future is more the result of random evolution than the result of organization—unpredictable chaotic interactions acting in constant adaptation to changing conditions. Modern society is defined by fluidity, learning, and constant reorganization. Librarians are faced with having to constantly reengineer their products and services to meet ever-changing demands. The problem is that they are trying to reconcile within their organizations (and themselves) these two competing visions of the future: planned and messy.

Libraries have traditionally done a reasonably good job of adaptation to changing circumstances, which had allowed them to remain viable. This has always happened largely in the context of the traditional hierarchy of a university campus. Basically libraries have been always been able to plan themselves out of trouble because events happened slowly enough that they had time to react. More importantly, they've always been able to figure out how to adapt: There's always been time to write another strategic plan or revise an existing one.

The question becomes, in a world with the rate of change and increase in the amount of information we now have, will libraries have that luxury in the future? How does a library deal with a world that is, fundamentally, chaotically messy, where the methods of technocratic planning are increasingly ineffective—even if there was time to do it? Libraries have always been able to function in the context of the idea that progress results in order—and that this order can be, somehow, predetermined and controlled—if only in some large strategic sense. How will libraries function in a world where this idea is no longer viable? How do you organize a library and its information in a world where the very idea of organization is seen as an obsolete concept?[34]

NOTES

1. Pongracz Sennyey, Lyman Ross, and Caroline Mills, "Exploring the Future of Academic Libraries: A Definitional Approach," *The Journal of Academic Librarianship* 35, no. 3 (2009): 252–59. Available from *Library Lit & Inf Full Text*, web (accessed May 13, 2011).

2. Frank Bass, "A New Product Growth Model for Consumer Durables," *Management Science* 15, no. 5 (1969): 215–27. Richard N. Foster, *Innovation: The Attacker s Advantage* (New York: Summit Books, 1986), 31, 103, 89–111.

3. Matthew J. Salganik and Duncan J. Watts, "Leading the Herd Astray: An Experimental Study of Self-fulfilling Prophecies in an Artificial Cultural Market," *Social Psychology Quarterly* 71, no. 4 (2008): 338–55. Available from *Social Sciences Full Text*, web (accessed May 13, 2011).

4. "Claude Chappe." Available from http://people.seas.harvard.edu/~jones/cscie129/papers/Early_History_of_Data_Networks/Chapter_2.pdf web (accessed September 21, 2011); Alexander J. Field, "French Optical Telegraphy, 1793–1855: Hardware, Software, Administration," *Technology and Culture* 3, no. 5 (1994): 315–47; Ronald Jones, "Terrorist Beheadings: Cultural and Strategic Implications," U.S. Army War College, 2005, 14. Available from http://www.dtic.mil/cgi-bin/GetTRDoc?AD=ADA434876&Location=U2&doc=GetTRDoc.pdf (accessed October 18, 2011).

5. Holy Bible, American Standard Version. Available from http://bible.cc/jeremiah/6-1.htm (accessed October 13, 2011); Polybius, *Histories*, book 1,

51, trans. W. R. Paton (London: W. Heinemann; New York: G.P. Putnam's Sons, 1922). For a further discussion of the philosophical implications of the Polybius example, especially in relation to the idea of education and learning, please see Arthur Eckstein, *Moral Vision in the Histories of Polybius* (Berkeley: University of California Press, 1995), 250 and ff.

6. Howard G. Brown, *Ending the French Revolution: Violence, Justice, and Repression from the Terror to Napoleon* (Charlottesville: University of Virginia Press, 2006), 338–50.

7. Waldemar Kaempffert, "War and Technology," *The American Journal of Sociology* 46, no. 4 (1941): 431–44.

8. Jan Morris, *The Oxford Book of Oxford* (Oxford: Oxford University Press, 1978), 224. For this concept expressed by Morris and the following paragraph see Ross King, *The Judgment of Paris: The Revolutionary Decade That Gave the World Impressionism* (New York: Walker and Company, 2006), 13–25, although the entire book is relevant to some extent.

9. Laura Otis, "The Metaphoric Circuit: Organic and Technological Communication," *Journal of the History of Ideas* 63, no. 1 (2002): 105–28.

10. Robert Sabine, *The History and Progress of the Electric Telegraph: With Descriptions of Some of the Apparatus* (New York: Van Nostrand, 1869), passim.

11. Iwan Rhys Morus, "The Nervous System of Britain: Space, Time and the Electric Telegraph in the Victorian Age," *British Journal of the History of Science* 33, no. 3 (2000): 455–75.

12. "1845: John Tawell, the man in the Kwaker Garb." Available from http://www.executedtoday.com/2010/03/28/1845-john-tawell-quaker-aylesbury/ (accessed October 10, 2011); "Not What He Seemed John Tawell of Berkhamsted—the 'Quaker' poisoner." Available from http://www.watfordobserver.co.uk/nostalgia/crimelibrary/johntawell/ (accessed October 10, 2011) and see http://www.oldbaileyonline.org/browse.jsp?id=t18480131-616&div=t18480131-616&terms=telegraph#highlight (accessed October 10, 2011).

13. Armand Mattelart, *Networking the World, 1794–2000* (Minneapolis: University of Minnesota Press, 2000), 6. For the comments and statistics in the preceding paragraph that relate to Mattelart's comments, see P. M. Kennedy, "Imperial Cable Communications and Strategy, 1870–1914," *The English Historical Review* 86, no. 341 (October 1971): 728–52; Daniel R. Headrick and Pascal Griset, "Submarine Telegraph Cables: Business and Politics, 1838–1939," *The Business History Review* 75, no. 3 (Autumn 2001): 543–78.

14. Bernard Lightman, *Victorian Popularizers of Science: Designing Nature for New Audiences* (Chicago: University of Chicago Press, 2007), 1–9, 19–24.

15. Richard Hack, *Hughes, the Private Diaries, Memos and Letters: The Definitive Biography of the First American Billionaire* (Beverly Hills, CA: New Millennium Press, 2001), passim; Tim Onosko, *Wasn t the Future Wonderful?: A View of Trends and Technology from the 1930s* (New York: Dutton, 1979), 138–39, 158–59, and passim.

16. Knut Hickethier, "Early TV: Imagining and Realising Television," in *A European Television History*, ed. Jonathan Bignell and Andreas Fickers (Oxford: Wiley-Blackwell, 2008), 55–78.

17. "Hughes Deplores Our Speed Mania," *New York Times*, October 10, 1923. Available from http://www.newyorktimes.com (accessed October 7, 2008); Clifford Stoll, *Silicon Snake Oil: Second Thoughts on the Information Highway* (New York: Doubleday, 1995), 1–4, 174–203.

18. "Rise of Radio Creates New Church Problem," *New York Times*, August 3, 1924; "Radio Seen as Aid to Religion," *New York Times*, September 12, 1926; David A Yallop, *The Day the Laughter Stopped: The True Story of Fatty Arbuckle* (New York: St. Martin's Press, 1976), passim; Stephen Vaughn, "The Devil's Advocate: Will H. Hays and the Campaign to Make Movies Respectable," *Indiana Magazine of History* 101, no. 2 (2005): 125–52.

19. "Charles Babbage." Available from http://www.oldcomputers .arcula.co.uk/hist3.htm (accessed October 15, 2011); Doron Swade, *The Difference Engine: Charles Babbage and the Quest to Build the First Computer* (New York: Viking, 2001), passim.

20. Ibid.

21. Swade, *The Difference Engine*, 296–307.

22. William Gibson and Bruce Sterling, *The Difference Engine* (New York: Bantam Books, 1991); "Steampunk." Available from http://secondlife.com/ destinations/roleplay/steampunk (accessed October 17, 2011).

23. Swade, *The Difference Engine*, 14–16; National Oceanography Centre, POL Technology History. Available from http://www.pol.ac.uk/home/oetg/ history.html (accessed October 17, 2011).

24. Jennifer S. Light, "When Computers Were Women," *Technology and Culture* 40, no. 3 (July 1999): 455–83; Stephane Groueff, *Manhattan Project: The Untold Story of the Making of the Atomic Bomb* (Lincoln, NE: iUniverse .com, 2000), 211–13.

25. Jurgen Rohwer, "Signal Intelligence and World War II: The Unfolding Story," *The Journal of Military History* 63, no. 4 (October 1999): 939–51; "History of Cryptography." Available from http://www.logicalsecurity.com/ resources/whitepapers/Cryptography.pdf (accessed September 21, 2011); Andrew Hodges, *Alan Turing: The Enigma* (New York: Simon & Schuster, 1983), passim and 158; F. H. Hinsley and Alan Stripp, *Codebreakers: The Inside Story of Bletchley Park* (Oxford: Oxford University Press, 1993), passim; Sharon Ghamari-Tabrizi, "Simulating the Unthinkable: Gaming Future War in the 1950s and 1960s," *Social Studies of Science*, 30, no. 2 (April 2000): 163–223.

26. Arthur L. Norberg, "High-Technology Calculation in the Early 20th Century: Punched Card Machinery in Business and Government," *Technology and Culture* 31, no. 4 (October 1990): 753–79; W. Boyd Rayward, "Library and Information Science: An Historical Perspective," *The Journal of Library History*, 20, no. 2 (1974–1987): 120–36; "Online Catalog and

Circulation: New Step for NELINET," *Library Journal* (November 15, 1980): 2370.

27. Robert E. Molyneux, *The Internet Under the Hood: An Introduction to Network Technologies for Information Professionals* (Westport, CT: Libraries Unlimited, 2003), 61–102 passim, and especially 82–102; William O. Scheeren, *Technology for the School Librarian: Theory and Practice* (Santa Barbara, CA: ABC-CLIO/Libraries Unlimited, 2010), 39–48.

28. Vannevar Bush, "As We May Think," *Atlantic Monthly* (July 1945): 261–78; G. Pascal Zachary, *Endless Frontier: Vannevar Bush Engineer of the American Century* (New York: The Free Press, 1997), passim.

29. Available from http://cs.ulb.ac.be/public/_media/teaching/infoh303/dbhistnotes.pdf (accessed September 21, 2011); Raúl Rojas and Ulf Hashagen, eds., *The First Computers: History and Architectures* (Cambridge, MA: MIT Press, 2000), passim; available from http://www.cs.umd.edu/class/spring2002/cmsc4340101/MUIseum/applications/spreadsheethistory1.html (accessed September 21, 2011); Edgar F. Codd, "A Relational Model of Data for Large Shared Databanks," *Communications of the ACM* 13, no. 6 (June 1970): 377–87; John Baker and Stephen J. Sugden, "Spreadsheets in Education The First 25 Years," Spreadsheets in Education (eJSiE) (2003). Available from http://epublications.bond.edu.au/ejsie/vol1/iss1/2 (accessed October 15, 2011). A more condensed history of spreadsheets can be found at D. J. Power, "A Brief History of Spreadsheets," DSSResources.COM. Available from http://dssresources.com/history/sshistory.html, version 3.6, August 30, 2004. Photo added September 24, 2002 (accessed October 15, 2011).

30. Greg Riccardi, *Principles of Database Systems with Internet and Java Applications* (Boston: Addison Wesley, 2001), 2–17, 71–92.

31. Nicholson Baker, "The Author vs. the Library," *The New Yorker* 72 (1996): 50–62.

32. K. Maloney et al., "Future Leaders' Views on Organizational Culture," *College & Research Libraries* 71, no. 4 (2010): 322–45, quote from 337.

33. D. B. Gaspar et al., "A Case Study in Collaboration: Assessing Academic Librarian/Faculty Partnerships," *College & Research Libraries* 70, no. 6 (2009): 578–90; M. Barry, "Research for the Greater Good: Incorporating Service Learning in an Information Literacy Course at Wright State University," *College & Research Libraries News* 72, no. 6 (June 2011): 345–48.

34. Karl Bridges, *Expectations of Librarians in the 21st Century* (Westport, CT: Greenwood Press, 2003), passim.

CHAPTER 2
Internet Insecurity

Modern libraries and the Internet have developed in an era of relative affluence and stability. For the last century the United States has been one of the world's most economically stable nations, as evidenced by the fact that the U.S. dollar is the de facto "world currency" universally accepted. This has consistently benefited American libraries, from Andrew Carnegie funding the construction of public libraries in the early twentieth century to post–World War II growth of higher education to the development of the Internet itself—the latter two events heavily subsidized by robust federal spending. There have always been enough economic resources to allow libraries to thrive, although clearly, considering their yearly budgets, many practicing librarians might disagree. The question remains: how would libraries function in an environment of real and continuing scarcity?

Libraries are subject to two kinds of disasters—natural and man-made. The first, such as an earthquake or hurricane, we can do little to mitigate against, except by having a robust and well-practiced set of emergency procedures in place. The second, man-made, reflects the possibility that in an economic recession, such as the one that started in 2008, libraries will receive less funding and be less able to serve their public. This is of particular concern in the area of electronic resources, where both kinds of events could have an impact.

AN EXERCISE IN INDIVIDUAL PREPAREDNESS

Let's say the lights go out right this instant as you're reading this at home. Where's your working flashlight? Don't know? Found it, but the batteries are five years old and it doesn't work? Realize you never bought a flashlight after the last one broke? Or you never bought one in the first place? Your neighbor borrowed it and never returned it? OK. You see my point. If you've answered in the negative for your own personal preparedness (and we're talking about just a flashlight, not whether you have a month's work of canned goods, a Big Berkey water filter, and an emergency medical pack in your house), imagine the complexity of the preparedness problem on an institutional and societal level. And in case you're wondering, I have six flashlights at home, two in my office, one in my car, a Coleman lantern, an oil lamp, and a box of 100-hour emergency candles.

Let's face reality; in the end we are responsible for ourselves and the institutions we have agreed to care for, including our students, patrons, and employees. It's nice to think that, in a disaster, someone will come quickly rolling up in some big truck to help us out, but the truth is that we will, for a longer or shorter period of time, be on our own and we better be ready.

THE DEATH OF A THOUSAND CUTS: THE ECONOMIC CONSEQUENCES OF DISASTER

It is easy to visualize the effects of direct disaster. A hurricane, such as those that struck the Gulf Coast in the 1990s, especially Hurricane Katrina, left an indelible set of images on the public consciousness. From the library perspective, it caused a massive amount of damage to libraries that will take years to repair. Natural disasters can drain money from public sector budgets. Money spent on fighting forest fires in the West, managing higher snowfalls in the Northeast, or paying for flood relief in the Southeast is money not available for library budgets. In these kind of situations, libraries could easily be seen as places where public investment can be postponed or canceled altogether.

SHOULD WE BE AFRAID?

A major terrorist or natural disaster event might cause a major disruption to the supply chain, such as imports of foreign products, which would have rapid and visible effects on the lives of average Americans who could, for example, quickly see the shelves of their local Wal-Mart and other stores empty of products. People preoccupied with obtaining the basic necessities of life are probably not going to be using libraries or supporting increases in their funding. Libraries have no control over these kinds of disasters, but in the area of their expertise, information technology, they can prepare for the eventuality that at least one scenario might threaten the basis of their modern operation: disruption of the Internet.

THE LIBRARY AS AN INTERNATIONAL BUSINESS

The Internet has made libraries vulnerable. Dependent on the Internet for the information resources needed to accomplish their daily tasks, from e-mail to online databases, libraries are now, for better or worse, Internet-based businesses, facing the same risks—viruses, malware, and network outages—that face companies. The very nature of the library enterprise, which focuses on open exchange of information, means that libraries are actually more at risk. By their nature libraries cannot easily and rapidly adopt the security mechanisms that would help them thwart problems, and, indeed, many of these issues are simply beyond the ability of the library to deal with. On a larger strategic level, libraries are also subject to international events that might disrupt the very functioning of the Internet itself.

Libraries are dependent on the continuing existence of access to a wide range of resources—from specialized minerals required for producing computer hardware to undersea cables to international agreements on Internet standards. All of these require, to some lesser or greater degree, a functioning and stable international community. The reality is that many countries in the world on which the Internet depends for basic resources—such as materials like cadmium, which is used in making of circuit boards—are not very politically stable places, such as Zaire.

Librarian concerns about security have been, traditionally, local and parochial. Concern about security issues tends to focus on physical security, such as preventing people from stealing the books or keeping the local flasher out of the stacks. As a profession librarians have not had a significant interest in international security affairs or much professional reflection on the impact of foreign events on their operations. This is understandable. Until the advent of the Internet, libraries had a limited amount of contact with entities outside their own immediate communities. Perhaps, worst case, some international crisis might delay the purchase or delivery of a foreign book or periodical, but that was about it.

The development of the Internet starting in the 1980s made all libraries international. For the first time libraries became integrated on an international level, with easy access to international catalogs and expedited communications with foreign libraries and material suppliers. This created an expectation among users that materials could be routinely obtained quickly and easily from the most obscure sources. This allowed libraries to radically restructure their own internal processes. Few academic libraries, at least larger ones, could contemplate doing business without access to WorldCat or other large international bibliographic databases.

Librarians have been slow to consider the implications of internationalization for library security. A September 2010 search of H. W. Wilson's Library Literature and Information Full Text found 192 articles mentioning "terrorism" with 33 mentioning "internet." A search on "librarianship international aspects" in the same database finds 790 articles, the majority discussing the positive aspects of this development such as cooperative projects between libraries in different countries and the value of the Internet in facilitating this. Librarians, as a profession, while apparently embracing the concept of the internationalization of their profession as a good, have spent correspondingly less time researching the security implications inherent with these developments.

HOW SECURE IS THE INTERNET?

Internet security is a major concern in discussing the future of libraries, because of both the risk to the infrastructure that libraries depend on as well as the costs involved in developing viable security strategies. In discussing Internet security, what I mean is widespread and long-term disruption. The Internet is now, essentially, a commercial operation. There's little profit in defense. The reality is that the points of physical vulnerability are both few and well known. A physical disruption of this network or, much more likely, an electronic disruption of the underlying software that runs the Internet—from either foreign or domestic sources—such as the DNS servers that convert understandable URLs into the numerical address the Internet needs to work, would be catastrophic. Government or military users can, for their part, depend on separate networking systems. The average library, on the other hand, is dependent on commercial service providers.

The possibility of increased and more serious cyberattacks is well recognized. In 2010 a federal report showed a 39 percent increase in cyberattacks directed at government websites from the previous year to over 40,000. A 2008 Heritage Foundation report makes the point:

Strategies must be national in character and international in scope. Nearly every domestic cyber program—from managing movement of goods, people, services, and ideas to controlling a border to investigating terrorist groups—requires international cooperation. This dimension of safeguarding the home front is nowhere more important than in addressing national infrastructure, supply-chain issues, and public-private partnerships. America is part of a global marketplace with a global industrial base. Virtually no nation is self-sufficient.[1]

PROTECTING LIBRARIES AGAINST CYBER THREATS

Illegal downloaders of music and other people who misuse the Internet are seen in the public eye as free thinkers who just want open access to information. The reality is much more serious. The kinds of hackers and criminals on the Internet are not teenage pranksters. They are highly sophisticated, are sometimes government backed, and have the ability to do tremendous damage.

Clearly, large portions of computer security are beyond the control of the library and are handled at the institutional level: firewalls, institutional licenses for virus protection, and the like. There is still a wide range of issues where the library can exert itself to create a more secure system. These include increasing hardware security, insisting on employees and patrons using secure passwords, and avoiding threats posed by "social engineering," e.g., educating both staff and patrons to avoid compromising their security through responses to bogus e-mails requesting sensitive data (known as "phishing").

From the standpoint of computer security, libraries operate in a conflicting environment. In order to be available to their users, including community users, they have to provide an open computing environment. However, this very openness also makes the system vulnerable to hackers, viruses, malware, and other system threats. Combined with a user population often ill educated in the risks of computer usage, this could be a recipe for disaster.

In their article "Wireless Network Security Issues," although not specifically discussing libraries, computer scientists Pardeep Kumar, Ashwani Kush, and Ram Kumar identify "identity," "access control," "authentication," and "confidentiality," among other issues that would be useful for librarians to consider in their work.[2]

Most librarians are familiar with the basic kinds of computer security threats, such as computer viruses. To a large extent these have been dealt with in many places, at the institutional level, by the development of firewalls, Internet intrusion detection systems, and automated scanning of e-mails to remove offensive software. More insidious is the development of Web 2.0 technologies, such as Facebook or other social networking sites, and the increasing availability of free "cloud computing" software and services, which allow users to keep their data and applications in remote locations on the Internet—places that may not have the well-developed security environment of their own campus environment. Seemingly simple and safe applications, such as Google Calendar, can become threats once users simply start adding attachments to their calendar entries, perhaps spreadsheets of secure information.[3]

Clearly, on a technical level, except at the larger institutions, the responsibility for network and computer security rests at the institutional level. Other than being zealous advocates for secure systems and making sure that institutional security directives are followed, there is probably little that librarians can directly do to create more secure systems; although, to be certain, librarians may have to reconsider (and be active participants in discussions about) development of more robust security systems. The use of individual personal characteristics for security such as fingerprint or retinal scanners may grate against traditional librarian (and societal) views on issues of privacy, but will become the norm.[4] Where librarians can be most effective is in education of users about information security. Users need to be educated about such threats as part of their basic information literacy education, and continual updating of information about such threats should be a regular part of library information efforts through RSS feeds, blogs, and other mechanisms used to connect with users. Librarians need to know the information habits of their users, especially in the realm of Web 2.0 technologies, and be able to communicate effectively with users about how to keep themselves secure.[5]

One neglected threat is simply the current trend toward going green. People are encouraged to recycle their used electronics, such as computers and cell phones. Although this is commendable from an environmental perspective, the reality is that many people toss their old cell phone in the e-recycle bin without bothering to erase the data on the device, data that can range from the merely embarrassing such as spring break vacation photos to the more serious, e.g., passwords, Social Security numbers, and credit card information. Libraries, as part of their education efforts, should encourage students to fully erase their old data.

PRIVACY IN THE ONLINE ENVIRONMENT

The larger issue this addresses is that of privacy. For about $6,000 you can buy a web-enabled refrigerator. Personally, I've always found the idea of my kitchen appliance knowing what's in it, by scanning the barcodes of the products on the shelves and automatically calling in an order when I run low on ice cream, somewhat Orwellian. We depend on the Internet to run many of those systems, such as surveillance cameras in public places, which are actually important in making us feel secure, if not, as in the case of a refrigerator, well fed. Note that I said "feel." Whether those systems actually do increase security is another issue entirely, but their absence would probably do nothing to enhance public confidence.

My personal observation is this: I have been in libraries that have surveillance cameras at their entrances. I'm not sure this deters crime, but it would seem to encourage users to be more polite to the circulation staff. One presumes that there is a similar "courtesy effect" in public spaces like airports and subway systems. As a culture we've accepted a level of surveillance and intrusion into our personal lives that previous generations would probably find appalling and that is seriously debatable from the standpoint of civil liberties, but its sudden absence would be disruptive if for no other reason than various agencies, such as the Transportation Security Administration, depend on computers and cameras and scanners and probably have few procedures, if any, to deal with their absence.

In the long term some widespread Internet event, such as a cyberattack, which would seriously affect the operation of the Internet, would inevitably trigger a discussion on a national level about Internet access that might force widespread changes in how the Internet is operated—for example, requiring the universal use of authenticated computing, e.g., some kind of national "Internet license" that would be required for users to log in or the widespread use of biometric scanning or Internet monitoring. In addition, the government would most likely require, in the interest of national security, severe restrictions on access and availability to certain technical information, with, quite possibly, the redaction or removal of many information resources that are now available. More importantly, there would be an overall shift in public opinion that could force the government to put more money into national security infrastructure, which might reduce funding for social programs such as education and libraries.

These events, in combination, could result in a fundamental shift in the way that libraries are viewed in society. This could have adverse effects on library content as libraries, desperate for public funding, attempt to make their collections as "inoffensive" and "safe" as possible. In a worst-case scenario, there could be a real erosion of traditional standards of library privacy and public access as the government attempted to control access to sensitive information along the lines of what was seen after 9/11, such as the U.S. Patriot Act, but revisited in an even more intense way.

HOW CAN LIBRARIES ENHANCE PRIVACY

Leaving technical issues aside, the most important thing that libraries can do is develop, publicize, and consistently enforce a well-written policy on privacy—not only of traditional issues, such as circulation records, which are often covered in many states by law, but also of privacy of user information gathered or kept by vendors. One by-product of the U.S. Patriot Act after 2001 is that many libraries are keeping less historical information, such as circulation records. They are also stepping up their efforts to ensure patron privacy. This is evidenced by the efforts of organizations, such as the American Library Association, to publish model draft language for libraries to develop effective privacy policies.[6]

Libraries, when possible, should endeavor to include privacy statements in their contracts with vendors. At a minimum, as part of a well-crafted privacy policy users should be advised to use care in their online activities. The language of the privacy policy of UCLA Library provides a good model for this:

The Library Web site links to other sites and services that are not contained nor controlled within the Library's online environment. Where the Library contracts with vendors for digital information products and resources, every attempt is made to include user privacy protections in the license agreements. However, the practices of these external sites are not under the control of the Library; thus, users are encouraged to read the privacy statements at those sites to learn of their privacy practices.[7]

Librarian researcher and expert on the U.S. Patriot Act Trina Magi has pointed out that we can't simply depend on the goodwill of vendors in protecting the privacy of patron information. Her research survey of

27 major vendors' privacy policies found that many were deficient when compared to privacy standards generally accepted by the library profession as a whole and major professional library organizations such as the American Library Association. While many vendors do a reasonably good job of explaining their policies, they are generally unclear on how that personal information will be used and/or distributed, or how users can control the use of their information once in possession of the vendor.[8]

NOTES

1. Available from http://www.heritage.org/research/reports/2008/12/building-cyber-security-leadership-for-the-21st-century (accessed May 5, 2011). http://www.security-technologynews.com/news/more-cyber-attacks-against-government-in-2010.html (accessed October 1, 2011). For a useful discussion of the supply chain issues, see Steven S. DeBusk, "What Happens When the Supply Chain Breaks? Implications for the Army Supply Chain Under Attack," US Army School of Advanced Military Studies, 2003 as well as Yossi Sheffi, "Supply Chain Management under the Threat of International Terrorism," *International Journal of Logistics Management* 12, no. 2 (2001): 1–11.

2. Ashwani Kush and Ram Kumar, *DESIDOC Bulletin of Information Technology* 25, no. 1 (January 2005): 14; Pardeep Kumar, Ashwani Kush, and Ram Kumar, "Wireless Network Security Issues," SCRA 2004-FIM XI, December 27–29, 2004, Institute of Engineering and Technology, Lucknow, India.

3. T. Cramer, " 'Maltweets' Pose Threat to Web 2.0 Users," *EContent* 32, no. 7 (September 2009): 12; B. Quint, "Cloud Foundations: Stability Issues in Third-Party Computing Platforms," *Information Today* 25, no. 7 (July/August 2008): 7–8.

4. M. Earley, "Are Biometrics the Key to Data Security?," *EContent* 29, no. 7 (September 2006): 38–42.

5. T. K. Huwe, "Mapping Your Digital Community in Five Steps," *Computers in Libraries* 30, no. 2 (March 2010): 26–28.

6. "Model Policy: Responding to Demands for Library Records," *American Libraries* 38, no. 8 (September 2007): insert 1–4. For an excellent review of the effects of the USA Patriot Act on libraries, please see Abby Goodrum and Velma Rogers, "Impact and Analysis of Law Enforcement Activity in Academic and Public Libraries," prepared for the American Library Association. Available from http://www.ala.org/ala/aboutala/offices/oitp/publications/booksstudies/LawRptFinal.pdf (accessed October 1, 2011).

7. Available from http://www.library.ucla.edu/privacy/index.cfm (accessed September 5, 2010).

8. T. J. Magi, "A Content Analysis of Library Vendor Privacy Policies: Do They Meet Our Standards?," *College & Research Libraries* 71, no. 3 (May 2010): 254–72. I would further like to acknowledge Professor Magi's helpful conversations and comment on some of my draft pages on this subject with me during the writing of this book which greatly clarified my understanding of privacy issues.

CHAPTER 3
Why Libraries Are Like Wal-Mart (and Not)

People are cheap. In general no one likes to spend more than they have to for anything. It's just human nature to try to optimize spending to get the most product for the least cost, which explains, at least in part, the popularity of Wal-Mart. This tendency of human nature is good for libraries—after all we provide the best product of all, knowledge, for free. With the advent of Web 2.0 technologies, we are able to get even better at what we do best—giving knowledge away. Libraries not only have begun developing an innovative technology that makes us more effective at providing value, but have also started developing new economic paradigms for library services. In an economy where success and influence are based on the ability to attract attention rather than on resource allocation of scarce physical objects, librarians have a unique opportunity to develop new models for library services—paradigms that can greatly raise the public perception of librarians as professionals and increase the profile and influence of libraries in society.

THE BASIC OF CLASSICAL ECONOMICS

People often tend to see many users of the Internet as being, basically, anarchists. Illegal downloaders of music are seen to be like Peter Fonda in the 1966 biker movie *The Wild Angels* who when asked "What do you want?" answered, "We just want to be free. We just want to ride our bikes and not be hassled by the Man." The truth is that users of the

Internet have reasonably well-developed theories of economics they are operating under—unstated, but existing nonetheless.

SCARCITY—WHY IT MATTERS

To understand this we need first to review some basics of Economics 101. A fundamental tenet of classical economic theory is the idea of scarcity. In a given area a limited amount of a good is produced, say, grain. In any given year there is a fixed amount of grain available in the market for sale, due to a variety of factors including weather, the decisions of farmers to plant, yields, and the flow of the finished product to other areas; e.g., if the farmer can get a higher price in the next county, he will withhold his crop from the local market thus raising prices. In classical terms, economics is based on the idea that there is a limited amount of any given produced good. Scarcity creates value.[1]

In the information economy, this becomes a different situation where scarcity is less a product of limits on production, e.g., the amount of grain that can be grown in a given area, than artificial limits such as copyright protection. There is a form of scarcity in that there are limited inputs available for the initial production of a product, but after it is produced the marginal cost of reproduction (the additional cost to produce 2 units or 20 or 5,000) approaches zero.

A commercial example of this is lala.com, which sells recorded music. This website lets users listen for free to any song one time. If you want to hear it again, you have to pay. This is a brilliant idea. There is a certain, probably large, percentage of people who never buy anything and simply use the service as a free jukebox; the costs of the service are offset by that smaller percentage of people who do purchase. Scarcity is less an issue of the amount of product than an artificial limit (one play per song) placed on the product by the vendor. The actual cost for the company of having 5,000 people listening to Mojo Nixon's "Elvis Is Everywhere" is probably not much higher than having only 1 person listening. The company, by attracting attention through its "free" business model, probably actually increases its sales. One can see the same thing in other companies, like Apple, which offers a large number of free "apps" in its online store right beside its paid products. The downside of this, of course, is that free is not always a viable business model. As of March 2011, lala.com is long dead.

The same kind of thinking operates in libraries. The oldest and most common example is, of course, books. Buy once, use forever—or until it gets worn out or stolen. Recorded music is another readily under-standable model for librarians. There are limits on the amount of recorded music that can produced, related largely to the initial costs involved in producing the music (building a recording studio, hiring studio engineers, finding musicians talented enough to create music that people will want to buy); this creates the costs for the final product. Once music is produced and available in a digital form, however, the per unit cost to the consumer becomes extremely low (99 cents on iTunes), ignoring, for purposes of argument, that the user has fixed and continuing costs of buying a computer, an Internet connection, electricity, and time.

Where does this lead? In classical economics, items have some kind of intrinsic value based on their perceived worth in the marketplace. In the case of land, for example, there is a limited amount upon which is imposed a commonly accepted system of valuation. Everyone can agree that a certain piece of property has value. There may be disagreement over this value, but, again, we have a system of appraisers who can be used to determine an agreed upon value for people involved in a transaction. In the electronic environment, we do not. Perception and attention of consumers drives prices, not some commonly accepted system of value determination. In the Internet marketplace, one can argue that the availability of information actually drives prices. I can find out the price of a product from 20 different vendors quickly and easily. More perfect knowledge creates a more perfect marketplace, thus lowering prices.

MARGINAL UTILITY

This is complemented by the issue of marginal utility, which, I would submit, is a fundamental difference between producers and consumers in a digital environment. Producers of digital content assert that their product has a marginal utility greater than zero past first sale, while consumers assert that the value of the product is zero. Physical products, regardless of circumstance, almost always have some kind of residual value. On the other hand, there are no junkyards for digital recordings where they can be sent to die and pressed into something else.

What matters to the majority of people in their estimation of value is functionality for the purpose they intend to use the product for, which is, ultimately, a matter of personal preference. In the case of cars, for example, for purposes of simply driving around town my 15-year-old car is fine. Perhaps not as nice as a newer, more expensive model, but it works. If I was planning an extended road trip in the near future, on the other hand, I might want to upgrade. The Internet world is different. Consumers of digital content, unlike, say, consumers of physical products such as pears, don't see any monetary worth to a digital product beyond the initial sale. They will use the mechanism of the Internet to find as much information as possible to get the lowest price. This may result in people being "legal" (paying money) or, in other cases, seeking free products through avenues such as music and movie piracy. We will ignore, for sake of argument, the minority viewpoint that all information should be free and assume that users, as a group, generally accept the idea of some form of capitalist marketplace.

THE ETHICS OF THE DIGITAL MARKETPLACE

Users of these peer-to-peer file-sharing networks don't see themselves as thieves in the sense of thinking they shouldn't pay for product, but have developed an economic argument that value ceases upon first sale and for producers to attempt to gain compensation beyond that is wrong. In some sense the modern teenager crouching in his bedroom with Napster or Kazaa has reestablished and extended the medieval concept of a "just price." As Thomas Aquinas stated:

If someone would be greatly helped by something belonging to someone else, and the seller not similarly harmed by losing it, the seller must not sell for a higher price: because the usefulness that goes to the buyer comes not from the seller, but from the buyer's needy condition: no one ought to sell something that doesn't belong to him.[2]

The fundamental argument that is routinely made is that consumers who download digital files without paying for them are guilty of theft. In a strict legal sense, this is true. However, it assumes that both the producers and the consumers share the same ethical system and agree on what constitutes an "unethical" act, which is much less the case. One could point to many reasons why different ethical viewpoints have developed, including the decline of religious values or lack of moral education, but one possible explanation lies in the idea of attention. As has been suggested elsewhere, we can be seen as entering what one could call an "attention economy." In the past, due to the paucity of mass media individuals were forced to take a wide view. One was educated to the idea that there was one set of values and, in practice, one had to take into account the views of the wider society in one's actions. Living in a small town, for example, one wouldn't routinely take up shoplifting because of both the limited number of things to steal and the overwhelming chance one would be caught. As a society we paid attention to the actions of others and adjusted our actions in accordance with the expectation (or perception) that lack of conformation with accepted norms would result in a penalty. In economic terms, there would be an opportunity cost, e.g., going to jail for not going along with the norm.[3]

In the modern digital economy, by contrast, everyone lives in the same large city where no one especially cares what people do. There are, of course, the screams from digital content producers, but the cry is lost in the overall hustle and bustle. In a world of constantly bifurcated attention, angst about the unethical behavior in relation to one single node is lost.

Ethical behavior matters more in an economy of scarcity. Ten individuals stranded on an ice floe will care more about the distribution of a limited amount of a nonrenewable food supply in an equitable manner (and the theft of that food) than the same group of individuals at a banquet at the Ritz Hotel. Abundance and autonomy beget sin. In this case what we're really talking about, as suggested above, is two things: the indifference of a group of users of digital resources to a commonly accepted societal norm, and the fact that, as a whole, society can't agree on what the commonly accepted norm is.

In the case of the Internet, the sheer numbers of users (combined with the ready availability of nexuses of access for both downloading and uploading information into the system) has created a situation where the group, fundamentally, creates its own law. A crowd of 10 people demonstrating on a street can be readily controlled by the police and a requirement for a permit. A crowd of 300,000 makes its own rules and enforces them on the larger society, including the cops. One only has to observe the situation surrounding most G-8 economic summits to see that this is true—to the point where these meetings of world leaders are now held in secure locations closely resembling armed camps under siege, e.g., Davos, Switzerland, rather than the heart of major cities like Seattle.

THE ATTENTION ECONOMY

Michael Goldhaber, noted commentator and writer on the developing information economy, has written extensively about the idea of an attention economy, suggesting that we convey meaning to an object or situation by paying attention to it. In the digital world, one can suggest, the idea of moral conduct regarding the use of digital materials can be seen to be influenced by this principle. The fact that usage of a digital resource is "illegal" is simply another meaning that users can choose to observe or, more often, ignore rather than a societal taboo. If one considers, for example, the downloading of a digital music file, there are numerous aspects, what we could call "leaves of attention," that users notice: do they like this artist; do they have a copy of this song; is the song something they want; is it of a size and file type readily downloadable; is it something that has been recommended to them to others? The fact that the very act of downloading may be illegal is simply one more nexus, one node, one leaf, on what one could refer to as an "attention tree." Value is created by meaning. So, in a situation where the meaning attached by one's attention is small (or nonexistent), the corresponding value associated with that "leaf"—monetary, moral, whatever—is small to nonexistent, just as when the first red leaf of autumn is swamped by the 99.9 percent of leaves that are still green, the red leaf is invisible.[4]

This leaves the question of why. What motivates the user of digital resources to take the risk, however small it may be in reality, to steal digital files and risk lawsuits, monetary damages, and, in short, incur opportunity costs for their actions? The Austrian scientist Georg Franck made a comment regarding scientific information that seems applicable:

Science is a collective endeavor: an industry in which the work of one set of specialists serves as input for other lines of specialized production. From a collective point of view, science can only function rationally by an efficient division of labor. If the available talents and efforts are allocated suboptimally, scientific production will not achieve collective excellence even if it is optimized from the viewpoint of the individual. But how are we to assess efficiency in science? Efficiency concerns the output into which resources that are used are transformed. But the output of scientific work consists of information, which is semantic and pragmatic in nature and thus defies immediate measurement. Scientific information even seems to escape economic valuation. Economic value is determined by the willingness of those interested in a particular item to pay for it. But the output of scientific production is not sold on markets: it is published. Publication puts intellectual property at the disposal of the general public under the sole condition that its processing into the intellectual property of the user is credited by citation. The performance of knowledge production can therefore not be assessed by comparing inputs and outputs in monetary terms.[5]

THE LEAVES OF ATTENTION OR ECONOMIC RATIONALITY
IN THE DIGITAL FOREST

One possible explanation: The downloaders are actually expressing an attempt to create a more rationally allocated set of nodes of attention. In a "legal" manner the distribution of these nodes, these leaves, is restricted by various legal mechanisms, most obviously by having them only available in security-coded shrink wrap in brick-and-mortar stores. The illegal downloading of music, then, can be seen as an attempt to redress this irrational, in the view of the users, allocation of resources. Illegal downloaders, in effect, are similar to individuals breaking into the grain silos of the farmers mentioned at the beginning of this piece and redistributing the grain where they feel it is needed.

Illegal downloads of music (or any other digital materials) are reflecting the principles expressed by Franck regarding scientific information. He stated: "Efficiency concerns the output into which resources that are used are transformed." Illegal downloaders are exercising this idea that, since in their view the system is inefficient in how it distributes information, this has created conditions of artificial scarcity. Their actions, while perceived quite correctly by majority moral and legal positions as being wrong, represent a kind of digital Benthamism where their actions, in their view, are creating efficiencies in the marketplace and thereby creating the greatest good for the greatest number, which in the end is what the idea of just price really comes down to.

Goldhaber makes the observation that huge numbers of postings on the Web or the net, along with many kinds of information distributed by more primitive means, never receive the slightest attention—that is, in the old terms they are not consumed; there is no demand for them. No matter how curious or inquisitive we may be, or how desirous of being entertained, there is already far too much information coming at us for us to make good use of it, or indeed to take it in at all. If the growth of material production was limited by the ability to consume, then the growth of information should have been limited even more, if the economic motives for that growth had been the same. In other words, the tremendous growth of the information sector is entirely irrational from the viewpoint of standard economics, carefully analyzed. A different explanation is required.

LIBRARIES AND THE ATTENTION ECONOMY

This leads to a fundamental issue facing libraries. Individual users of digital resources have been attempting, legally or not, to create efficiencies in the marketplace. Libraries, on the other hand, have been attempting, with lesser or greater success, to accommodate all information being produced. Over the past 20 years we've seen an increase of great proportion to include all the new digital materials being produced as well as postprocess existing materials into some form of useable digital content, e.g., the Google book initiative.

This is all well and good, as long as one accepts the traditional definition of a library as an archive or a place where all the leaves of attention will be gathered and organized. But this leads to the question, assuming Goldhaber is correct, as to whether this strategy is wrong. Are libraries collecting materials that are used or simply materials that may never be used?

THE UNSUSTAINABILITY OF CURRENT LIBRARY ECONOMIC MODELS

The truth is that the present economic situation for libraries is unsustainable. Unlike the normal consumer in the marketplace, who is picking and choosing what items meet his need for attention, libraries assume that every node is of interest, at least potentially, so it needs to be collected or, at least, an access point defined. The former, from an economic perspective, is actually being more efficient. He knows he wants copies of all the Britney Spears songs in existence and can choose to ignore all the other nodes of attention competing against that. Libraries, by their nature, are being required to pay attention, to a lesser or greater degree, to all the leaves of attention. Libraries, from an economic perspective, are irrational since they are not seeking to maximize their economic efficiency except, perhaps, in some narrow sense of making broad collection decisions (we will not collect books written in Ge'ez) and economically (we won't buy the $100,000 database and will try to get discounts on the rest). The obvious problem in this situation, which is woefully familiar to every librarian, is that we have replaced onetime costs, e.g., a book purchase, with continuing (and everescalating) ongoing costs—often for the same materials in electronic format. Let me ask you librarians: is this working for you? I, like many librarians, see that the present state of library budgets is on a direct collision course with economic reality.

Libraries, as a practical matter, cannot pay attention to everything, to every node, to every leaf on the tree of knowledge. In the past we could, as a group, make at least the pretense of doing so. Now, even that polite fiction is denied us in the overall flood of information—for no other reason than we operate in conditions of scarcity of money, staff, and, most important, attention. There must be a new paradigm that deals with this reality.

HOW WEB 2.0 CAN HELP LIBRARIES

Web 2.0 is one approach to the problem. This can be seen as an attempt by librarians to involve themselves more fully into this economy of attention. Through creation of multiple points of interaction with users, the result is an increase in the level of attention paid by the user, compared to the static nature of Web 1.0 technologies, which were mostly passive in regard to the users. The result is what could be referred to as "multiple leaves of attention." Like the autumn tree of our earlier example, instead of one red leaf, there are a multitude with varying colors and shades.

More importantly, Web 2.0 also represents an attempt to deal with the issue of scarcity of library resources by making the users partners with the librarians in the creation and development of content. From an economic perspective, this is sensible since the library, aside from infrastructure costs of building and maintaining the system, is offloading the actual labor costs of selecting products to the users themselves.

There is, of course, major anxiety among library professionals, somewhat if not entirely justified, in doing this. For example, the library is giving up quality control and its monopoly over such things as the content of library catalog records by allowing user inputs. Presumably, although this is yet to be demonstrated by a substantial body of research, this will be offset by higher user participation and satisfaction. To some extent there is criticism of some Web 2.0 social networking activities, such as user tagging of catalog records, as being duplicative and unneeded since librarians long ago solved such issues with the use of MARC records and controlled vocabulary. However, understood from the standpoint of an attention economy, such activities serve to increase the public participation in and engagement with the library. The real question becomes not whether libraries will participate, but how they will shape this participation to meet their own needs and the needs of their users.

It would also seem, based on the experience of other professions, such as journalism or computing, that the widespread participation, the "democratization of" if one will, in information provision in economic terms, thereby eliminating a barrier to entry, should create a larger market for librarians through the creation of new forms of professional activity. For example, allowing readers to annotate the catalog with their impressions of read books eliminates the need for the librarian to provide reader's advisory services. Whether this is indeed the case that this leads to new and higher forms of professional activity (and recognition) or whether it results in the marginalization of librarians remains to be seen.

It does seem clear, however, that at present the advent of Web 2.0 services, instant messaging, and chat has resulted in a higher public profile for librarians and a greater amount of attention through the perception, especially by younger users, that librarians are "cool" or "hip."[6] More to the point, however, the advent of these services tends to raise the public awareness of librarians at exactly the same point in time, as illustrated by the discussion about ethics above, where librarians can exercise their existing moral and professional influence to help direct the development of new paradigms of thought. Rather than being simply marginalized as the archivers of existing content, librarians can participate front and center in the development of new technological models for access and distribution of content and, in the process, influence the moral and ethical development of society associated with such developments.

HOW CAN THIS BE ACCOMPLISHED?

There are a number of immediate steps that librarians can take to start making the changes suggested above happen:

- Librarians should implement the full integration of new technologies such as blogs as a format and, more importantly, with librarians as participants.
- Librarians need fuller engagement with the wider intellectual life of academe, perhaps by becoming more of a public forum for academic events, especially those related to issues of ethics and technology. The library as a community center of culture will have to become the norm for libraries to remain viable in a culture saturated with multiple media striving for attention. Public libraries have embraced this concept more readily than academic libraries.
- Librarians need to be seen as public intellectuals. Librarians need to be more fully engaged in public discourse, even in those kinds of venues that, traditionally, they

may have shunned. There is a place for librarians on talk shows or in print articles in newspapers and other places that people outside of libraries use.

- There needs to be more and better dialogue with users to develop collections that meet their needs rather than the expectations of librarians as to what libraries should be.

Most importantly, and this may be the most difficult thing to do, libraries will have to be focused. No longer can we attempt to be all things to all people, but rather need to concentrate on what our users need. It is this mind-set, moving from the librarian as expert in information to the librarian as coparticipant in a process of discovery, that may be the most difficult for many libraries (and librarians) to accomplish, but it is not impossible.

WHAT CAN WE LEARN FROM WAL-MART?

This is an analogy that may offend some people. Libraries after all are not businesses. They do have businesslike attributes and problems, the most important of which, from the public service viewpoint, is to get customers and keep them. Libraries are not, and in my view should not be run like, McDonald's. In some sense that is one of the worst attributes of modern universities. We have, in some cases, a class of professional administrators who may have never actually worked in a library telling us what to do, applying whatever outdated models they remember from their business school classes to the university (and libraries) without adapting them to our unique circumstances. In some sense librarians are like combat-hardened marines being led into battle by some nonqualified Pentagon bureaucrat who has never even handled a rifle. This is a recipe for disaster. That doesn't mean, however, that we can't take some pointers from the business world. So, what can we learn from Wal-Mart?

Libraries need to have lots of stuff. More to the point, we need to have it organized in a consistent fashion so our users can find it. To that end a modest suggestion: quit messing about with our interfaces—both our local websites and our databases. Sometimes change is good. More often, it just confuses people. I like the fact that my local Wal-Mart still has the sporting goods section in the same place.

VOX POPULI VOX DEI

This twelfth-century statement from Alcuin is often misquoted as "The voice of the people is the voice of God" or what people want is what they should get. Now, in the interest of accuracy I should point out that the correct quote is "Nec audiendi qui solent dicere, Vox populi, vox Dei, quum tumultuositas vulgi semper insaniae proxima sit" or "And those people should not be listened to who keep saying the voice of the people is the voice of God, since the riotousness of the crowd is always very close to madness." I disagree with Alcuin. Librarians should listen to the insanity of the mob. They aren't mad. They're right.

Libraries need to have the things people need. This means moving to a patron-driven model for collection development. Wal-Mart has great systems for tracking what sells and what doesn't. This probably explains why they don't carry much rockabilly music. Libraries have, for better or worse, operated on the assumption that the experts, e.g., the librarians, know what their patrons need better than the patrons. Libraries need to listen better, and this is exactly where appropriate use of Web 2.0 technologies can make us more effective. We can know, for the first time, what people really are using and what they really want and respond to that.

Note that I've said "appropriate." Libraries, unfortunately, tend to be in what might be considered a Web 2.0 arms race. There is no one-size-fits-all solution. Just because chat reference works in one library does not mean it will be beneficial in all libraries. Libraries should pick and choose what works for their situation and not be overly influenced by the current obsession with "best practices." Do what's right for your users.

What's the one thing we can learn from Wal-Mart? That we need to treat the patrons right. I can't go into my local Wal-Mart without tripping over someone in a blue vest wanting to be helpful. That's not to say that they are universally knowledgeable. In some ways Wal-Mart employees are like Google. They know where stuff is. They don't know everything about every product. They may or may not be able to advise on whether a product will meet our needs. In some sense they share the basic problem of librarians: there's simply too much stuff for any of us to truly know our collections anymore. Maybe we'd be better off having smaller, well-focused collections rather than trying to add piles of stuff. Do you know how much of that expensive e-journal collection you bought last year was actually used?

SELLING THE LIBRARY TO SKEPTICS

This leads us to marketing. Libraries have always operated with some sense of entitlement. They've been the only game in town. That's no longer the case. The information monopoly is over. There are an infinite number of information resources available to library users. Unless libraries make a compelling case to their users why they should use the library rather than some other source, libraries will cease to be relevant. Libraries need to have a coherent and effective marketing plan. More than that, they need to have a culture that encourages users to be there. That's why the survey tools that are available, such as LibQual, need to be used and the results acted on sensibly. The fact that people want something doesn't mean we need to make it so, but we do need to make use of what people are saying.

SURRENDER TO WIN

To some extent modernity means we have to simply concede some issues, such as food, noise, and cell phones, and just move on. We need to show flexibility on the small stuff. A young lady brought her bicycle into a library I worked in one day. She should have parked it outside. I talked with her and found out that it was her roommate's bike and she didn't have a lock. I looked in my office and found my spare bike lock. I loaned it to her. Problem solved. I won't see that lock again, but that's OK. The point is that that young lady went away really happy with the library and will come back. Alternatively, I could have yelled at her, quoted rules and regulations, and escorted her and her bike outside. I can pretty much guarantee in that scenario that that young lady would stay out of the library, forever. At the very least, even if she came back to the building, she would have a poor impression of the library—and, more than likely, communicated that to 50 of her closest friends. I'm not advocating chaos throughout the library, but some kind of controlled anarchy, like allowing the first floor to be a noisy communal study space, would probably be easier on everyone. Concede some territory and you can keep better control over the larger parts that truly matter.

That's not to say that librarians haven't always been helpful. In recent years, however, there's more and more a trend to use some electronic medium, such as e-reference or chat reference or a web page. We've cut our reference desk hours to be more cost effective. The reality is that students want to see a person. Students can lurk in their rooms behind their computer screens and instant-message a librarian, but part of an education, I would suggest, is learning to interact with people. Asking questions and interacting with strangers is a life skill. If you're a shy student or have little practice articulating a question clearly, interacting with a librarian is valuable. At some point students will be in job interviews or gainfully employed and being able to communicate effectively will be an extremely useful skill. And, for what students are paying for an education they deserve the services of a librarian, even on the weekend. We should be seen.

NOTES

1. W. Ellis, *The Classical Theory of Economic Growth* (New York: Palgrave, 2000), passim.

2. Saint Thomas Aquinas, *Summa Theologiae* (New York: McGraw-Hill, 1964).

3. Available from http://firstmonday.org/issues/issue2_4/goldhaber/ (accessed April 1, 2011).

4. Available from http://www.well.com/user/mgoldh/attmean.html (accessed April 11, 2011).

5. Available from http://www.sciencemag.org/cgi/content/full/286/5437/53 (accessed April 11, 2011).

6. K. Jesella, "A Hipper Crowd of Shushers," *New York Times*, July 8, 2007. Section 9, p. 1.

CHAPTER 4

Do Books in Libraries Have a Future?

With the development of electronic media and the Internet, the issue of whether paper books and other printed information sources will disappear is a matter of public interest. One only has to consider what the advent of the Internet has done to newspaper circulation sales to understand this. A paper medium which, in the 1950s, was the dominant method by which people got their information has been largely supplanted, even within the newspaper industry itself, by websites and blogs. Indeed, the idea of newspapers has dropped from popular culture.

As one example, take the movie *Hell and High Water* (1954) starring Richard Widmark and (a regrettably underrated) Bella Darvi. In the beginning the disappearance of a noted scientist is shown by a series of newspaper headlines; indeed, the opening sequence shows a car driving away from the front of the *International Herald Tribune* office where that day's issue of the newspaper is on prominent display in the front window being eagerly perused by a passerby. In 2011 this reference to the newspaper as an important element in daily life would not only be seen as inaccurate but as laughable. Even contemporary movies with newspaper themes, with the exception of such classics as *All the President s Men*, focus less on the issue of the newspaper as medium than on the personal lives of the various characters who happen to work for newspapers. The idea of the newspaper as a medium that reflects the wider culture as a relevant information medium has been largely removed. Indeed, it is doubtful that we will ever again see a major motion picture where a newspaper or newspaper journalist is the major plot element unless the movie is historical.

Will paper books, like newspapers, decline into extinction?

THE NATURE OF READING

To answer this question we need to first examine why people read. By understanding the different reasons that people read books, we can then examine the emerging technologies and see whether, indeed, the paper book, as we currently understand it, has any long-term future. People read for reasons that are, ultimately, personal and not subject to analysis. It is possible though, for purposes of discussion, to categorize the reasons individuals read into four primary groups: survival, work, community, and personal. The best way to understand this is to examine the typical day of a reading person. I will use myself as an example.

Survival reading can be defined as that reading that people use simply to negotiate their way in the world. For example, in simply driving to work today, I had to engage in several different acts of reading. On the way out the door I saw my gas bill, which upon inspection I realized was due and had to be paid. When I got in my car I had to read my gas gauge to see that I, indeed, had enough fuel to get to work. I stopped at my local fast-food restaurant and went through the drive-through where I had to read the menu. When I arrived on campus I had to read the notice in my customary parking lot telling me I had to park elsewhere because the lot was going to be paved. The printed book is fairly irrelevant to these kinds of activities, although, to be certain, I find it useful (and comforting) to have a printed copy of my auto's operating manual in my glove box.

Upon arriving at work I, of course, find printed books everywhere—since I work in a library this makes perfect sense. The vast majority of my communication needs are handled by e-mail, but I regularly use printed books as well. Although most of my book reading consists of traditional printed books, I find, more and more, that I do make use of electronic books—largely, however, for purposes of looking up specific facts rather than reading large chunks of text.

As a reference librarian I work in a mixed environment of materials, as do most academic librarians in libraries of any size. A large portion of the material is electronic, such as web pages and databases, while, at the same time, a great deal of the works are legacy materials, mostly books, that, for reasons of space, cost, time, or lack of interest by publishers, have not been converted into electronic format. To some extent the library, at least in the area of reference services, preserves some of its archival function; however, year by year paper materials represent a smaller and smaller proportion of the entire reference collection.

Indeed, in an electronic environment the whole idea of a "reference collection," in the sense that it has been traditionally envisioned as a particular localized collection, seems to become increasingly irrelevant. As a profession librarians have already seen particular formats within the reference collection, such as microfiche, be replaced and physically removed from the reference collection by the advent of electronic substitutes.

Obviously, there are many jobs where books are completely irrelevant to accomplishing work and others where books are even more essential. For instance, if my job involved climbing around the insides of jet airliners doing electrical repairs, I might find it useful (and necessary) to have book content on some form of electronic reader and/or have the paper manuals on a trolley available for quick reference. Lawyers represent a middle condition. They make extensive use of books while also making heavy use of electronic databases and online articles. In fact, the very codification of the law can be seen as one reason for the legal profession to exist as it does. To simply find a particular law, much less interpret it, requires specialized training. The development of a system of law books, many of which are difficult to use and understand even by librarians with specialized training, can be seen as an improvement in any previous system. Someone working in a toll booth, on the other end of the spectrum, aside from a paperback novel to pass the time, would have little or no need to refer to any books.

This isn't to suggest a classist approach to reading; e.g., the upper intellectual classes make use of books while the working class doesn't. It just is an accurate description of how work exists in the world. Reading books for work exists on a continuum from where it is very required and structured on the one end to where it is totally unnecessary on the other.

After work I stop at my wife's church for the evening service. Here I find myself, with religious texts and hymns, using books for purposes of community. Although this church is somewhat technologically progressive, projecting the lyrics for the various hymns on an overhead projector, I find it faster and easier to use the printed books in my pew. It is the case that using the printed books, along with the other members of my congregation, reinforces my personal feelings of being a member of a faith community. Put simply, I find it comforting and familiar to use a printed book in this context.

When I finally arrive at home in the evening, I find myself reading books for pleasure. It's not that I couldn't read much of the same material in an electronic format (I have an e-book reader), it is just that I find the act of reading a paper book to be both convenient and necessary—in the first instance because both the format and clarity of the printed book suits my needs, e.g., to be comfortable as opposed to sitting in front of a computer screen, and because the content I am interested in isn't available in an electronic format.

One can easily see that there simply isn't one mode of reading, but several different ways that people transition back and forth from throughout their day. An individual tends to choose the format of their reading to suit their individual needs and circumstances. The question then becomes, assuming that individuals behave in this manner, what would be the characteristics of the technology that would push them in one direction, e.g., toward the paper book, or the other, e.g., toward the use of an electronic substitute? And, we will assume that we are unbiased in terms of what device we use in the latter instance.

E-BOOKS AND THE FUTURE OF READING

The newest and most important development in the book world is the development of the electronic book. While, from a library standpoint, this is an emerging form—roughly in the same stage as electronic journals were 5 or 10 years ago with no generally accepted standards, varying formats, and a chaotic pricing structure—the rapid introduction into the consumer marketplace of a variety of e-book readers from many vendors makes it clear that the e-book format is here to stay and may, indeed, become the dominant force in the publishing industry.

Before we discuss the positive aspects of the e-book and its effect on the future of libraries, we should make one thing clear. Regardless of the potential growth of the e-book market, paper books are not going to go away. From the library perspective, there is simply too much of a capital investment in paper books to be abandoned. It should also be recognized that many books simply will not make the transition to electronic format, despite the best digitizing efforts such as Google Books, because of lack of funds, lack of interest, or scarcity. There are many books that, for whatever reason, have never made it into a library to be available to be digitized. Remember also that we are discussing books and leaving aside the entire issue of the digitization of journals. In large part this is a much more mature development, as the existence of large e-journal collections such as JSTOR attest, but there are probably an enormous number of fugitive publications that will escape digitization.

The other important point is that many people, despite the existence of e-book readers, like paper books. They are easy to use, comfortable to handle, and a widely accepted medium—perhaps the most accepted medium—for the public at large. People like their books and are not going to give them up for an electronic reader regardless of the quality of the product. In addition, of course, one needs to recognize that in many emerging countries, paper books are simply the only practical format. One is not going to see an e-book reader in some remote African village with low a per capita income and no electricity because of issues of price and lack of infrastructure.

On the other hand, although it is beyond the scope of this book, the case of Africa presents an interesting case in that, unlike developed nations, it basically skipped the technology of the twentieth century. Potentially, one could see a scenario where Africa becomes among the most advanced places technologically simply because they are starting from scratch and not having, as is the case in the United States or Europe, to adopt new technologies within an existing infrastructure. One only has to consider the issues in the United States with the switch from analog to digital television to see an example of the extra cost and complexity such a transition presents.[1]

THE HISTORY OF THE E-BOOK READER

Despite numerous attempts to create a successful product it has only been since the mid-1990s that technology and consumer economics have coincided to make e-book readers something with wide public acceptance. From the 1940s onward, people have considered the concept of being able to transfer the reading experience of paper books to an electronic environment. It was only in the 1980s, with the advent of CD-ROMs, that some form of electronic text became widely available and used. In the early 1990s primitive commercial products, such as the Sony Data Discman , entered the marketplace to limited commercial success. Other products that attempted to combine the idea of e-book reading and other electronic tools in personal digital assistants, such as the Apple Newton, met an equally cool reception, largely for issues of technology (size and short battery life), high cost, and lack of content. The focus of electronic texts throughout the 1980s and into the late 1990s was on the Internet, first with simple online text through electronic bulletin boards and later enhanced with the development of the World Wide Web and Internet browsers.[2]

THE INFORMATION-SEEKING BEHAVIORS OF MODERN STUDENTS

The reality of modern academic library users, especially those 18 to 20 years of age, is that they no longer, as previous generations of students did, see the library as the sole or, indeed, even a valid source of information. Thus one can see, by simply entering many academic libraries a ramping up of training efforts, i.e., "information literacy," as well as revamping and rethinking of the library environment through the establishment of new models of library services, such as the "information commons," designed to integrate library services with teaching and, in general, a de-emphasis on the idea of the "traditional" library policies such as bans on food and drink through the opening of cyber cafés. In sum, libraries are repositioning themselves within the academic environment to maintain relevance. The introduction of new formats, such as the e-book, is happening within this larger framework of redesign. This whole process is complicated by the fact that the business of the library cannot stop while this process is ongoing.[3]

The information-seeking behaviors of students still involve the library. They have a high degree of confidence both in their ability to use the resources and in the accuracy of the online materials they find. As library researchers O'Brien and Simmons correctly comment:

While librarians may view research along a linear, straightforward path...our emerging knowledge of Next-Gens indicates that they maneuver through information in multi-faceted, multi-source routes. It will be important to work with this reliance on one-stop shopping environments—rather than in opposition—to ensure that their research habits mature with some structure and they develop necessary critical thinking skills.[4]

The growth of the e-book format is not taking place in a vacuum but is being shaped by the user community, which is younger, often more technologically facile and adaptable than the teachers and librarians serving them, and more willing to accept ambiguity and "good enough" rather than demanding precise authoritative answers to questions. For a generation that takes questioning authority and risk taking as guiding principles, the idea of the librarian and the library, indeed academe itself, insisting on their traditional roles as the arbiters of knowledge seems increasingly outdated. The reality is that the modern student learns faster, learns differently, and uses that information in different ways than any previous generation. The question for librarians is how we can continue a relevant conversation with our own smarter children.

WHAT ARE THE CURRENT ADVANTAGES AND LIMITATIONS OF THE E-BOOK?

In this environment of change, how does one assess the potential of the e-book? One could argue the technological issues of e-books: they need electricity or wireless access, or the screen resolution is not very good on many models. These are excellent points, which we will explore further. It can be suggested, however, that the primary problem with e-books is the lack of useful content.

The fact is that paper books have been around a long time. E-books, on the other hand, haven't developed the same body of works available. On the consumer front, through major retailers such as Barnes & Noble and Amazon, there are a reasonable number of e-books available, but they, for the most part, are more recent and popular. The Amazon Kindle as of July 2010 offered 630,000 books plus 1.8 million out-of-print titles. The body of scholarly books in electronic format is a small proportion of this whole. Additionally, in many instances, unlike the case for consumer e-book products, e-books for the academic marketplace are often sold in bundles. One ends up buying 100 reference titles to get the 10 or 15 one actually wants. The overall trend is that e-books are increasing their market share at the expense of paper books, especially in the professional marketplace, such as computer programming books, where rapid outdating is the norm and users tend to use the books as reference materials rather than reading them in totality. In academic libraries, products such as Safari (focused on computer books) have been very successful in this niche area, but this has not yet extended to collection development in other areas to the same extent.

A 2009 survey of library users at the University of Illinois at Urbana-Champaign confirms this point:

E-books have gained a lot of traction with Library users and, taken along with our publisher usage statistics, show that e-books have become an important service offering for the Library. Clearly our users are interested in using more of this content, but great challenges lie ahead in terms of making this content available and providing improved search and discovery.[5]

E-BOOK USAGE IN AN ACADEMIC LIBRARY: USER ATTITUDES AND BEHAVIORS

It appears that the acceptance rate of e-books among academic users is high. The results of the UIUC study are confirmed by other research. A 2010 study of e-book usage focusing on medical texts found yearly increases in e-book popularity with the demand for paper texts being static; however, the latter were still being consulted with regularity. There are clearly obvious advantages in a medical environment for e-texts, which, unlike their paper counterparts, can be regularly updated. In particular it was found that the use of e-books was especially pronounced in the area of reserves, which has special implications for academic libraries in that reserve operations represent a significant operating expense in staffing, collection maintenance, and maintaining copyright compliance. This research parallels and confirms the experience of general academic libraries, which, as previously mentioned, have found a higher degree of acceptance of e-texts in technical areas, such as computing, as opposed to the humanities where print is still the dominant format.[6]

The growth and influence of e-books in the academic marketplace is moving at a slower pace, perhaps due to the traditional conservatism of many faculty to adopt new teaching modes or issues of expense. Faculty and students seem responsive to e-books for leisure reading, just noting from the present author's personal observation of the use of Kindles and other e-reading devices on his own campus. The situation regarding the criteria for the widespread adoption of e-books on campus was neatly summarized in 2008 by ECAR Fellow and Digital Content Strategist for the National Association of College Stores Mark Nelson, who identified five important points related to for e-book growth and acceptance which are worth quoting directly word for word from his article:

- Within five years, today's K–12 students will be showing up at colleges and universities with substantively different cultural attitudes towards e-books than today's students.
- A commercially viable e-reader will be on the market.
- New learning technologies are nearing the tipping point of maturity.
- Standards for e-books are emerging.
- IP issues will be mostly resolved either through technology (DRM) or business models.[7]

Colleges and universities, in most cases, have well-stocked libraries (in size if not in quality) and are loath to disregard this capital investment. The library has been the traditional center of campus life based on its monopoly on the book, and although that is rapidly changing in many academic libraries with the implementation of the learning commons model and integration of different services such as writing in the disciplines and other initiatives, the reality of many academic libraries is that they will be faced with the challenges of adopting this new book model and maintaining their existing paper collections, especially in areas where digitization is impractical or uneconomical (rare books are a good example of this), and funding these new initiatives. This situation is further complicated by the fact that within the next 10 years many, if not most, of the librarians currently working in academic libraries will retire. While this presents a great opportunity for libraries, and for those people interested in working in libraries, it also means a "brain drain" of experienced librarians just at a time when e-books will come to maturity as a format.[8]

THE ECONOMICS OF E-BOOKS FOR LIBRARIES

One way to consider the college or university is to use a business model; e.g., compare academia to a corporation. In many respects higher education, as pointed out by British economists Hare and Wyatt, does have aspects of a business. It takes in revenue, it has fixed costs (electricity and infrastructure) and variable costs (health care for employees), and there are management and employees (and sadly often conflict between the two just as in corporations, and, even more unfortunately, sometimes downsizing as programs are eliminated). Higher education also produces product—graduates and research. Of course, this analogy goes only so far. When one looks at the idea of a return on investment, for example, one may see little use for many departments, such as classics, English, or linguistics, except to the extent that research in those fields adds prestige to the institution and is part of the overall mission of the university. English majors, with few exceptions, rarely end by endowing their alma maters with rich endowed chairs.

The advent of e-books represents an opportunity to reduce many of the costs associated with higher education, such as textbooks. This is one of the first areas in which higher education sees a significant use of e-books, simply because of the costs involved for both the students who must buy the textbook and the school that must operate bookstores to sell them. It is possible to formally model the economics of a university from the standpoint of inputs and outputs, and obviously significant cost savings are in the interest of all parties. For a more detailed discussion of this topic, I recommend reading the technical appendix of the article by Hare and Wyatt, which lays it out all quite nicely.[9]

The economics of the introduction of e-books are complicated by the economic downturn, starting in 2008 which greatly reduced university funding. While to some extent this reduction in funding can be dealt with through the introduction of austerity measures within university operating budgets, there is a point where there is no fat left to trim and materials budgets will begin to be adversely affected. This economic downturn makes the introduction of new formats difficult, but, interestingly, in the next two years the expectation of resource expenditure cuts on e-books is less than that of other formats such as monographs and databases. This seems to show that librarians recognize the need to adopt the e-book format to remain competitive and relevant to their users. The upside of this situation, if it can be seen to have an upside, is that the economic downturn did force libraries and vendors to come to agreement on some limitation on the ever-escalating costs of serials—with increases of 6 to 8 percent expected in 2011. Whether this is a trend that continues remains to be seen, and based on past experience it seems unlikely, but it does give libraries, to a limited extent, the potential ability to reallocate materials funds to other formats such as e-books.[10]

Books do clearly have a future in libraries and in society in general. They will be different in format, in content, and this has serious implications for libraries in terms of how they deliver services and products to their users. As librarians we are confronted with an entirely new set of challenges in this new format. At the same time it offers us as a profession a great opportunity to develop new models of service and interaction with our public which can enhance the status of libraries as centers of cultural and intellectual life to the communities we serve.

NOTES

1. STT Netherlands Study Center for Technology Trends and Jasper Grosskurth, "Futures of technology in Africa." Available from http://www.stt.nl/uploads/documents/192.pdf (accessed October 5, 2011).

2. Marie Lebert, "A Short History of ebooks." Available from http://www.etudes-francaises.net/dossiers/ebookEN.pdf (accessed October 3, 2011) and http://ireadiwritepublishing.wordpress.com/2011/03/18/the-40 -year-history-of-the-ebook/ (accessed October 3, 2011); Stephen Segaller,

Nerds 2.0.1: A Brief History of the Internet (New York: TV Books, c1998), 264–80 although the entire book is relevant to the topic.

3. Pamela Harland, "Toward a Learning Commons: Where Learners Are Central," *Teacher Librarian* 38 (2011): 32–36; although Harland is using a high school as a model, the issues raised in her article are worth considering for academic libraries, and it seems a good short introduction and case study of the concept. C. Leeder, "Surveying the Commons: Current Implementation of Information Commons Web sites," *The Journal of Academic Librarianship* 35 (2009): 533–47; Ruth Kifer, "Real University Libraries Don't Have Neon Lights," in *Last One Out Turn Off the Lights: Is This the Future of American and Canadian Libraries?*, ed. Susan E. Cleyle and Louise M. McGillis, 47–63 (Lanham, MD: Scarecrow Press, 2005). Admittedly, this example from George Mason is somewhat older but it remains one of the better examples of how libraries are implementing these changes.

4. Heather O'Brien and Sonya Simmons, "The Information Behaviors and Preferences of Undergraduate Students," *Research Strategies* 20 (2007): 409–23.

5. Wendy Allen Shelburne, "E-book Usage in an Academic Library: User Attitudes and Behaviors," *Library Collections, Acquisitions, and Technical Services* 33, no. 2–3 (2009): 59–72, ISSN 1464-9055, 10.1016/j.lcats .2009.04.002. Available from http://www.sciencedirect.com/science/article/ pii/S1464905509000311 (accessed October 3, 2011).

6. Pamela S. Morgan, "The Impact of the Acquisition of Electronic Medical Texts on the Usage of Equivalent Print Books in an Academic Medical Library," *Evidence Based Library and Information Practice* 5 (2010): 5–19

7. Mark Nelson, "E-Books in Higher Education: Nearing the End of the Era of Hype?" Available from http://www.educause.edu/EDUCAUSE+Review/ EDUCAUSEReviewMagazineVolume43/EBooksinHigherEducationNearing/ 162677 (accessed April 14, 2011).

8. Denise Davis, "Library Retirements: What we can expect." Available from http://www.ala.org/ala/research/librarystaffstats/recruitment/ lisgradspositionsandretirements_rev1.pdf (accessed October 6, 2011).

9. Paul Hare and Geoffrey Wyatt, "Economics of Academic Research and Its Implications for Higher Education," *Oxford Review of Economic Policy* 8, no. 2 (1992): 48–66.

10. David Nicholas, "The Impact of the Economic Downturn on Libraries: With Special Reference to University Libraries," *The Journal of Academic Librarianship* 36 (2010): 376–82; K. S. Henderson et al., "Seeking the New Normal: Periodicals Price Survey 2010," *Library Journal* 7 (2010): 36–40.

CHAPTER 5
The Future of Libraries

The future of libraries will depend on a combination of the ability of librarians to adapt and remain flexible and the use of modern technology in the face of a rapidly mutating legal and economic environment. The development of new formats such as e-books, the increased costs of electronic resources, and the challenges of dealing with increased legal restrictions, such as limitations on the availability of fair use, will create a more challenging operational environment for libraries. The expected coming wave of retirements of librarians, which will take from many libraries a vast store of knowledge and experience and leave many libraries, if not understaffed, at least with more inexperienced librarians making decisions, will greatly add to the challenges that libraries will face.

LIBRARIAN RETIREMENTS—THE NUMBERS GAME

The age cohorts of librarians can be seen to skew slightly older than might be the case in other fields where, typically, one might expect workers to begin employment in their early or mid-20s right after finishing their undergraduate degrees. Figure 5.1 demonstrates the overall effect of this:

The complicating factor for library managers in the future decade will be the coming wave of retirements of academic librarians. As Table 5.1 shows, the period from 2010 to 2019 will show the loss from the

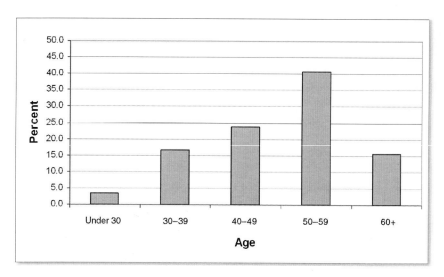

Figure 5.1 Credentialed Librarians by Age 2005. *Source:* Available from http://www.ala.org/ala/research/librarystaffstats/recruitment/Librarians_supply _demog_analysis.pdf, p. 9 (accessed March 17, 2011).

workplace of around 48,000 librarians—this from an initial estimated base of 106,000—amounting to about 45 percent of all currently working librarians.

The result of this will be, most likely, a tendency for academic libraries to offer the same services (or enhancements—such as Web 2.0 services such as instant messaging, etc.) with fewer people. Even if they hire

Table 5.1 Demographic Trends for Librarian Aging.

Number of Librarians Reaching Age 65 (2000 Census Base)	
Time Period	**Number**
2000–04	5,479
2005–09	12,898
2010–14	23,208
2015–19	25,014
2020–24	14,400
2025–29	8,674
2030–34	6,517
2035–39	5,544
2040–44	691

Source: http://www.ala.org/ala/research/librarystaffstats/recruitment/recruitretire-adeeperlook -figures.pdf (accessed October 7, 2011).

replacements, an iffy proposition perhaps given the state of reduced library budgets, new hires will certainly have less experience. If economic conditions make current librarians work longer, there will be an increased age skewing of the working librarian population. While this is, in general, not a bad thing—60 seems the new 40 in some sense with current advances in health and medicine and it will give libraries the benefit of experienced librarians for a longer time—it still leaves the questions of whether the student population, not to mention younger librarians, will relate well to older librarians and if those experienced librarians will be adaptable and amenable to the introduction of new technologies and service models.

ADAPTATION IN HIRING

Libraries are going to be required to be more adaptive in their hiring processes in order to get workers.[1] In the past it may have been the case that libraries could be somewhat particular in their choice of employees and had the option to take as long as needed to hire someone to fill an open position. In a new and competitive environment with a smaller pool of workers, who have skill sets in demand in other, higher-paying industries such as computing or information technology, libraries, while not lowering their standards, will be required to accommodate their hiring practices and working environments to the needs of a different kind of workforce.

One can usefully observe that perhaps younger employees will be more mobile, more inclined to want balance in their work and personal lives, and much less tolerant of having to endure poor working conditions. It may have been the case in the past that in order to keep a job, people were willing to put up with poor working conditions. In the future that seems much less likely. People can and will leave a job for any number of personal and professional reasons or none at all. The burden will be on the employer to attract *and* keep employees. As a 2006 article examining the issue of younger employees concluded:

These findings seem to suggest that there are significant differences between the attributes most highly valued by a number of academic library directors and by the Gen-X librarians. The latter appear to place more value on maintaining a balance between one's job and personal life and they frequently stress the importance of a person- or employee-oriented workplace that values teamwork, fairness, and loyalty.[2]

GETTING INSIDE THE DECISION CYCLE OF LIBRARY USERS

The fundamental issue for survival of libraries today, given these changes in library resources and staffing, is adaptation. In the modern information environment, the basic criterion that determines the success or failure of a library is the ability of the library staff to effectively adapt their policies and procedures to the needs of the user. On a daily basis we see users with technologies and skills that often exceed that of the library staff. The use of cell phones is a perfect example. This is widely used and accepted technology, but the response of libraries has been, in many cases, to limit the use of cell phones or ban their use completely. Cell phones are a symptom of a deeper problem—the inability of the library to adapt to change. In many cases, as most librarians will attest, libraries are woefully behind the curve.

It seems that a fundamental issue has been ignored by libraries—at least in a formal way: the lack of understanding of the Observation-Orientation-Decision-Action (OODA) loop. This lack of knowledge and use of this concept places libraries at a perpetual disadvantage compared to other organizations that have made use of the concept. Increased awareness of this cycle would benefit libraries by making them able to adapt better and faster to the needs of their users and, more importantly, allow libraries to better articulate their reactions to change. When combined with a basic knowledge of game theory, the result for libraries can be more optimal outcomes in a wide range of areas from operational questions to strategic planning.

THE OODA CYCLE—THEORETICAL EXPLANATION

The concept of the OODA cycle was first developed in the 1970s for military applications. The originator of the theory, Colonel John Boyd, in an analysis of air-to-air combat outcomes postulated a scenario in which one side in a conflict presented the other with a sudden, unexpected challenge or series of challenges to which the other side could not adjust in a timely manner. As a result, the side with the slower response was defeated, and it was often defeated at only a small cost to the victor.

In Boyd's paradigm, victors consistently are able to recycle through the OODA loop, or Boyd Loop, faster and this gave them an advantage over their adversaries. The actions of the opponent, on the other hand, became slower and slower. Since they were going through the OODA loop slower, over time they fell further behind until the faster side achieved victory. This model, although originally applied to military situations, is also applicable to business and other competitive situations.

Boyd postulated that any conflict could be viewed as a duel wherein each adversary observes (O) his opponent's actions, orients (O) himself to the unfolding situation, decides (D) on the most appropriate response or countermove, then acts (A). The competitor who moves through this OODA-loop cycle the fastest gains an inestimable advantage by disrupting his enemy's ability to respond effectively. He showed in excruciating detail how these cycles create continuous and unpredictable change, and argued that our tactics, strategy, and supporting weapons' technologies should be based on the idea of shaping and adapting to this change—and doing so faster than one's adversary (see Figure 5.2).

The ability to understand the orientation function is the key to success because it allows a competitor to penetrate his opponent's decision cycle. Each of us bases our decisions and actions on observations of the outside world that are filtered through mental models that orient us to the opportunities and threats posed by these observations. These mental models, which the philosopher of science Thomas Kuhn called "paradigms," shape and are shaped by the evolving relationship between the individual organism and its external environment.

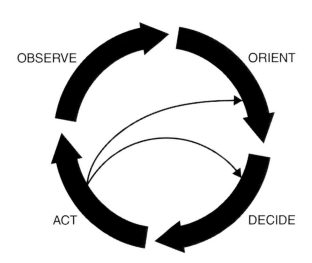

Figure 5.2 The Observation, Orientation, Decision, Action Cycle (Boyd Loop). *Source:* G Frederick Thompson, "Business Strategy and the Boyd Cycle," *Journal of Contingencies and Crisis Management* 3, no. 2 (June 1995).

In a 1997 article published by the U.S. Naval Institute, Franklin C. Spinney, a close associate of Boyd's, summarized the essence of the Boyd Loop theory:

In conflict, each participant, from the individual soldier trying to survive to the commander trying to shape strategy, must make decisions based on his orientation to reality—his appreciation of the external circumstances which he must act on. Boyd argued that one's orientation to the external world changes and evolves, because it is formed by a continuous interaction between his observations of unfolding external circumstances and his interior orientation processes that make sense of these circumstances. These interior process take two forms activity: analysis (understanding the observations in the context of pre-existing patterns of knowledge) and synthesis (creating new patterns of knowledge when existing patterns do not permit the understanding needed to cope with novel circumstances).[3]

The synthetic side of the dialectic is crucially important to one's orientation, because it is the process by which the individual (or group) evolves a new worldview, if and when one is needed to cope with novel circumstances. But as Kuhn has shown, the synthetic process can be extremely painful, because its nature is to build a new paradigm by destroying the existing one. Boyd strove to use multiple, quick-changing destructive thrusts to isolate his adversary from reality by destroying his existing paradigm, and at the same time, deny his adversary the opportunity to synthesize a new paradigm. The combination of menacing pressure and an inability to cope with external circumstances causes the adversary to experience various combinations of uncertainty, doubt, confusion, self-deception, indecision, fear, panic, discouragement, and despair—which, in turn, overload his capacity to adapt or endure.[4]

IMPLICATIONS OF THE BOYD LOOP FOR LIBRARIES

Libraries are recognized for many things, such as good service to users, interest in issues of intellectual access, and use of technology. What libraries are not always noted for is speed. In some cases libraries are slow to respond to the changing needs of their users. One particular example is the use of interlibrary loan. Now, first, let the reader not think that I, as a librarian, am critical of interlibrary loan. It is a valuable service and the people who work there work very hard indeed.

The reality of interlibrary loan, however, is that it is sometimes slow. This isn't to say that there are not rush services. However, it often takes a week to several weeks to get an item for a student. In many cases, telling a student they need to wait two weeks is tantamount to telling them the item is unavailable. There are various responses to this situation. The student can go to the local Barnes & Noble and purchase the book. Often, especially in larger cities, the book is either readily available at the store or can be delivered within a day or two. This response is a perfect example of the Boyd Loop. Given the library reaction to the request—e.g., wait two weeks—the student got inside the decision cycle of the library, reacted, and in this case the library, in effect, was defeated in that the student obtained his materials outside the library.

A library response, in turn, to this situation that would get inside the decision cycle of the student would be to offer overnight delivery comparable to the bookstore or, even better, to offer the book online. The ultimate response would be, of course, to have detailed information regarding the student and anticipate his request prior to his even asking—for example, a system of electronic reserve that ties into the university registration system or the professor's syllabus and automatically sends the student the required reading when they need it, e.g., the night before the material is discussed in class.

There are obvious implications in that this, and many other library activities, can be seen as dynamic noncooperative games. For example, collection management decisions, especially activities such as periodical reviews, can be seen the same way in that there are several players seeking to maximize their self-interest, the results of which can be expressed in a variety of ways—including a Nash equilibrium solution.[5] What these examples illustrate is that libraries already use the Boyd Loop in their operations. There are mechanisms, of lesser or greater formality, in every library that make use of the concepts of the Boyd Loop. Librarians simply don't recognize that they are using it and, in consequence, are not using the mechanism to their fullest advantage.

ANTICIPATION AS THE KEY TO SUCCESS

In the illustrations above, the use of the Boyd Loop dealt with a practical issue of materials delivery. In many cases the response of libraries tends to be reactive. For example, people bring in their cell phones. This is seen as a problem because they can be loud or disruptive. Policies are put in place saying "No cell phones." Students end up unhappy because they can't use their phones. Staff is unhappy because they feel they have to be "phone police" and are not doing what they really want to do. Using the Boyd Loop, the library could have anticipated the issue and created a better outcome.

The key to success is anticipation. With the proper awareness of the emerging technology, a library could anticipate that a new technology will become important. The library could then process this information and get inside the decision cycle of students, perhaps by creating quiet areas in the library, asking students to silence their phones when not in use, or even installing soundproof phone booths (with appropriate signage) for users. The time to do this is before the technology hits a critical mass of users. Trying to regulate the technology after everyone has adopted it will be inefficient, and, in any event, by that point the next decision cycle by users will have begun for the next wave of technology, e.g., wireless laptops. The library is left behind. Fundamentally, what we're talking about here is an inability of libraries to react quickly to novelty.

ADOPTING THE BOYD LOOP APPROACH: PRACTICAL SUGGESTIONS

Libraries can be relatively slow in their decision-making processes. They can also tend to be policy driven. The usual approach to a situation is to (1) identify the problem, (2) decide if a policy is needed, (3) develop the policy, and (4) implement the policy. This all takes time. It also reflects a top-down management structure as far as decision-making processes are concerned. In some cases libraries have adopted a team-based approach to management where the decision-making process is decentralized from central administration and left in the hands of team members. However, this is sometimes not an improvement, especially if teams are large and develop cumbersome internal procedures for responding to problems.

In either case the real issue is the lack of speed. Any decision-making process takes time. As an organization the library is at a distinct disadvantage against individual users because their decision-making process is more flexible and faster. Libraries have to and should reduce barriers to timely decision making. Regardless of the increases in efficiency of the internal mechanisms of the library, their decision-making process will never be faster than that of the user due to the reasons stated above. Despite this libraries could do a better job of reducing the barriers to quicker decision-making processes and thus get inside the decision loops of their users somewhat faster by use of information.

It should be pointed out that this chapter tends to use technology as an example of the Boyd Loop and its implications, largely because this is relevant and understandable. The fundamental principles being discussed here could, however, also be usefully applied to other areas of library operations with equal utility. For example, it also could apply to human resources where the internal mechanisms of the hiring process are in competition with the decision-making process of the applicant. The job applicant can speedily choose between job offers A, B, or C in a time frame much faster than the library, as an organization, can make the hiring decision. The applicant is inside the decision loop of the organization and therefore comes out ahead. In a broader sense, this can also be seen in terms of the competition between libraries for personnel, or even in terms of the competition of libraries as a whole for personnel against related businesses, such as the computer industry, that are competing for the same people—the implication being that libraries with more streamlined and faster hiring processes will be at an advantage in the marketplace compared to their slower competitors.

Libraries, since they do have the inherent disadvantage of being, often, larger organizations, can compensate somewhat through the use of strategic intelligence. Institutional changes, especially in the area of technology, tend to be slow. This reflects the complexity of technological infrastructure, the costs involved, and the various levels of administrative bureaucracy that exist. In the area of technology, there is also a trade-off between innovation and stability. Libraries tend not to be first adopters of new technology. They also tend to keep technology longer, e.g., keeping computers until they literally fall apart.

In terms of technology, then, to get ahead of the decision curves of their users libraries need to adopt a more proactive and less risk-neutral approach to technological innovation. This does not mean, necessarily, that libraries have to adapt wholesale change every time a new technology develops. Libraries should be aware of the trends in new technology, especially in terms of their users' needs; be willing to invest regularly in technology on a research and development basis; and be willing to invest not only in hardware and software but in human resources and planning for future development. Such an approach implies a greater integration of the library operation, especially in the area of technology, with other campus units such as academic and administrative computing. This doesn't mean a merger of these organizations, but does suggest a sharing of expertise and a willingness to disregard the traditional political and social boundaries between libraries and other technology innovators on the campus would be beneficial. By doing so the library (and the campus as a whole) starts operating within the Boyd Loop at a higher and more effective level. The fundamental driving force behind the Boyd Loop is information. The more you know about your adversary (or your patron) and what they plan to do the more effective you can be. By combining the expertise and information from different areas, the library/computing complex attains a gestalt that allows them, as a whole, to move closer into the OODA loop of their users, thus assuring a higher chance for successful outcomes.

IMPLICATIONS OF BOYD LOOP THEORY FOR MANAGEMENT ANALYSIS

The real value of the Boyd Loop is that it gives organizations a method of analysis for determining where they are failing and succeeding in serving their users. It provides a concrete method of discussing, as was mentioned earlier, what up to now has been understood largely by intuition. If, for example, you know that the entire freshman class is bringing laptops and your response the summer before is to install a wireless network, you have been operating in a Boyd Loop. Essentially, what we're talking about here is vocabulary. It's not that libraries have done such a bad job overall. What we've been lagging behind, perhaps because of our focus on users and day to day events, is articulating what we're doing and why—not only to ourselves but also often to shareholders outside our immediate group. We react to external circumstance without any real reflective analysis of what the reaction actually means. In sum, what we have going on is a kind of unexamined evolution of process. We act without being actually aware of the motivations of why we act. The use of Boyd Loop analysis provides a methodology for having a meaningful discussion about library activities and processes, placing them in the larger context of the organization as a whole.

BOYD LOOP THEORY IN THE CONTEXT OF GAMES: IMPLICATIONS FOR PLANNING

If one considers library activities, as suggested earlier, as a form of noncooperative game, then one can see, as Hallett suggests, that the outcome can be considered an open-loop decision where the decision is based on the player's information set, which is based on a variety of factors including realized values of past variables, expectations of future variables, and dynamic economic responses. Boyd Loop theory is, at its core, about the collection and assimilation of information. In the context of games, therefore, the use of Boyd Loop theory represents a methodology for evaluation of those variables mentioned above in a more efficient manner as well as a mechanism for creation of future responses.

Modern library strategic planning is informed by numerical data. The decision-making process is largely normative. That is to say, despite the presence (or absence) of data, the end result of strategic planning processes tends to be subjective. There are usually empirical data from which these metrics can be gathered, e.g., increase in number of patrons served, increase in number of materials owned, or some other measure of increase in efficiency. This results in a decision matrix—of lesser or greater complexity depending on the environment and level of analysis—on the basis of which future decisions are taken. The issue for libraries is that, although the decision matrix is based on metrics, it is not, nor should it be, derived only from them, but also from subjective factors. In many cases, these subjective factors have not been subjected to a high degree of analysis—often because of the lack of a tool for that process, e.g., the Boyd Loop. The result can be planning decisions that are inconsistent, especially in terms of the overall institution if the library fails to take into account the larger organizational mission or the diverse needs of multiple stakeholder groups—students, faculty, administrators—all with different needs and perceptions.

Where the system sometimes also breaks down is in the level of cooperation between the library and other campus units, especially those at a higher level. The errors of subjectivity in the decision matrix are compounded on an institutional basis since, normally, the strategic planning process is centrally controlled and administered across units in a uniform manner—or at least an attempt is made towards that centralization. In practical terms what usually happens is, in effect, the outcome of the process is considered by the participants to be a zero-sum game where one participant's gains come at the expense of the other's equivalent losses. The use of Boyd Loop theory, in conjunction with the idea of noncooperative games, could provide a useful mechanism for libraries to analyze their planning processes and result in more optimal outcomes. Much more research remains to be done in this area.

THE PAST AND FUTURE OF LIBRARIES

Rigid in their approaches and selection of subject matter, universities were for centuries often centers of reaction, introverted and hostile to the introduction of the sciences into the curriculum. It is only from the early nineteenth century, with the creation of Berlin University in 1809, that modern universities developed (with an emphasis on research) graduate education, stressing the authority of the professor. Various attempts at university reform, in both Europe and the United States, by century's end led to the development of the modern American research university. The establishment of modern schools such as the University of Michigan and Johns Hopkins University marks important milestones in the development of the contemporary American university, especially in the concept of the system of elective courses, which is the basic organization still widely used today.[6]

AMERICAN HIGHER EDUCATION SINCE 1945 AND LIBRARIES

In the post–World War II period, American universities and colleges saw a marked increase in their student populations. In 1945 there were 2.3 million students enrolled in 1,768 institutions. These numbers rapidly increased in large part due to the federal subsidies provided to returning veterans under the GI Bill. This trend continued through the remainder of the century, aided by a combination of growth in economic affluence where a college education became seen as a standard experience for middle-class households, an increase in the opportunity of women and minorities to attend college, and, perhaps most importantly, increased federal support for higher education. By 1980 there were 3,231 institutions enrolling 12 million students, with the number of earned degrees growing from 10.7 million in 1970 to 29.9 million in 2010. Trends in college enrollment are projected to exceed 20 million by 2020.[7]

A combination of legislation, such as the 1963 higher education facilities act for the construction of residence halls, libraries, and research buildings, was accompanied by an increased flow of government funding to fields, especially the sciences and engineering, seen as important in helping the country in the developing post-1945 Cold War. This trend was especially noticeable after the successful Russian orbiting of the first Sputnik satellite in 1957 led to an almost panic mentality among the general public and government officials that the nation was losing scientific superiority. These increased ties to federal funding were accompanied by a strengthening of relationships between higher education and business interests. Previous ideals of the university as existing largely for the public good—education for education's sake as it were—became deemphasized with an increased focus on producing outputs useful to industry, e.g., research results focused on and graduates trained in scientific/business areas, and the widespread adoption by higher education of business management practices and goals. Higher education became a place where competition rather than contemplation became more and more the norm, especially among public universities which trended towards increased state control and centralization marked by the creation of state systems designed to rationalize and increase economies of scale, especially in the areas of administration and physical facilities.[8]

The higher education establishment of the early twenty-first century has transformed in purpose and function and, in some respects, is indistinguishable from corporate entities, with a focus on marketing, competing with other universities for students, and numerical measures of outputs and productivity throughout the organization. The implication for libraries is clear. They have to become more efficient and faster organizations that better meet the needs of their users who, saturated by information overload on an almost 24/7 basis, also have many alternative resources ranging from Google to commercial e-resource vendors. The question is how we do this without losing the very values that make libraries important to users—the library as place, a welcoming environment, and maintain its traditional role as a center of campus life. This is our challenge, mission, and a great opportunity.

NOTES

1. Wendy Arant Kaspar and Pixey Anne Mosley, "Making the Good Hire: Updating Hiring Practices for the Contemporary Multigenerational Workforce—Part Two: Library Administration and Management," *Library Leadership and Management* 22, no. 3 (Summer 2008): 142–47; Karl Bridges, *Expectations of Librarians in the 21st Century* (Westport, CT: Greenwood Press, 2003), passim.

2. Arthur P. Young, Peter Hernon, and Ronald R. Powell, "Attributes of Academic Library Leadership: An Exploratory Study of Some Gen-Xers," *The Journal of Academic Librarianship* 232, no. 5 (Summer 2006): 501.

3. Franklin C. Spinney, "Genghis John," *Proceedings of the U.S. Naval Institute*, July 1997. Available from http://www.usni.org/magazines/proceedings/1997-07/genghis-john (accessed October 6, 2011). I will point out that there are various descriptions of Boyd's paradigm—"OODA" and "Boyd Cycle." I have chosen to use the term "Boyd Loop" based on an article by Berndt Brehmer who uses the term "Boyd's OODA Loop." Available from http://www.dodccrp.org/events/10th_ICCRTS/CD/papers/365.pdf (accessed October 8, 2011). One also sees alternative terms such as "OODA Loop." Available from http://www.army.gov.au/lwsc/docs/Thomas_Abandoning_the_Temple.pdf (accessed October 8, 2011). There seems to be

a variety of usages in the literature so I have adopted "Boyd Loop" as a reasonable paraphrase of these various usages.

4. Available from http://des.emory.edu/mfp/Kuhn.html (accessed October 7, 2011)—an excellent study guide and outline of Kuhn's major work *The Structure of Scientific Revolutions* by Professor Frank Pajares of Emory University. Also Kuhn's primary work itself: Thomas S. Kuhn, *The Structure of Scientific Revolutions* (Chicago: University of Chicago Press, 1970), passim.

5. For a discussion of the dynamics of this situation as it relates to game theory, see A. J. Hughes Hallett, "Non-cooperative Strategies for Dynamic Policy Games and the Problem of Time Inconsistency," *Oxford Economic Papers* New Series, 36, no. 3 (November 1984): 381–99, especially 383. Unfortunately, the library literature on the use of game theory is limited. See Zhong Ying and Aaron Hegde, "Applying Game Theory in Libraries: Review and Preview," *Library Philosophy and Practice.* Available from http://www.webpages.uidaho.edu/~mbolin/zhong-hegde.htm (accessed October 24, 2011). See also Spinney, "Genghis John," 42–47. *Proceedings of the U. S. Naval Institute*, July 1997, 42–47. I am most indebted to Professor G Frederick Thompson of Willamette University, who gave me permission to use the figure of the Boyd Loop in Figure 5.2 from his article "Business Strategy and the Boyd Cycle," *Journal of Contingencies and Crisis Management* 3, no. 2 (June 1995): 81–90. For an overall discussion of the history and development of the theory, the definitive source, at present, is Robert Coram, *Boyd: The Fighter Pilot Who Changed the Art of War* (Boston: Little, Brown, 2002). The literature is somewhat limited since during his lifetime, Boyd consistently refused to articulate his theory in publication, preferring to offer an intensive multihour (or multiday) briefing.

6. James Turner and Paul Bernard, "The German Model and the Graduate School: The University of Michigan and the Origin Myth of the American University," in *The American College in the Nineteenth Century*, ed. Roger Geiger, 221–41 (Nashville, TN: Vanderbilt University Press, 2000); Frederick Rudolph, *The American College and University: A History* (New York: Knopf, 1968), 264–86, 329–72.

7. Arthur Cohen with Carrie B. Kisker, *The Shaping of American Higher Education*, 2nd ed. (San Francisco: Jossey-Bass, 2010), 188; "School Enrollment: 1980 to 2020." Available from http://www.census.gov/compendia/statab/2012/tables/12s0219.pdf (accessed October 11, 2011); "Higher Education Institutions and Enrollments." Available from http://www.census.gov/compendia/statab/2012/tables/12s0278.pdf (accessed October 26, 2011); "Educational attainment by race and Hispanic Origin 1970 to 2010." Available from http://www.census.gov/compendia/statab/2012/tables/12s0229.pdf (accessed October 26, 2011).

8. Clark Kerr, *The Great Transformation in Higher Education, 1960–1980* (Albany: State University of New York Press, 1991), passim; Jonathan R. Cole, *The Great American University* (New York: Public Affairs, 2009), 145–74.

Further Reading

Anderson, Chris. 2006. *The Long Tail: Why the Future of Business Is Selling Less of More*. New York: Hyperion.

Aspray, William. 1990. *John von Neumann and the Origins of Modern Computing*. Cambridge, MA: MIT Press.

Au, Wagner James. 2008. *The Making of Second Life: Notes from the New World*. New York: Collins.

Auletta, Ken. 2009. *Googled: The End of the World as We Know It*. New York: Penguin Press.

Banks, Michael A., and Orson Scott Card. 2008. *On the Way to the Web: The Secret History of the Internet and Its Founders*. Berkeley, CA: Apress.

Barabási, Albert-László. 2010. *Bursts: The Hidden Pattern behind Everything We Do*. New York: Dutton.

Baron, Dennis E. 2009. *A Better Pencil: Readers, Writers, and the Digital Revolution*. Oxford: Oxford University Press.

Berners-Lee, Tim, and Mark Fischetti. 1999. *Weaving the Web: The Original Design and Ultimate Destiny of the World Wide Web by Its Inventor*. San Francisco: HarperSanFrancisco.

Bielefield, Arlene, and Lawrence Cheeseman. 2007. *Technology and Copyright Law: A Guidebook for the Library, Research, and Teaching Professions*. New York: Neal-Schuman.

Boureau, Alain, and Roger Chartier. 1989. *The Culture of Print: Power and the Uses of Print in Early Modern Europe*. Princeton, NJ: Princeton University Press.

Buinicki, Martin T. 2006. *Negotiating Copyright: Authorship and the Discourse of Literary Property Rights in Nineteenth-Century America*. New York: Routledge.

Burke, Colin B. 1994. *Information and Secrecy: Vannevar Bush, Ultra, and the Other Memex*. Metuchen, NJ: Scarecrow Press.

Bush, Vannevar, James M. Nyce, and Paul Kahn. 1991. *From Memex to Hypertext: Vannevar Bush and the Mind s Machine*. Boston: Academic Press.

Campbell-Kelly, Martin. 2003. *From Airline Reservations to Sonic the Hedgehog: A History of the Software Industry*. Cambridge, MA: MIT Press.

Carr, Nicholas G. 2008. *The Big Switch: Rewiring the World, from Edison to Google*. New York: Norton.

Ceruzzi, Paul E. 1983. *Reckoners: The Prehistory of the Digital Computer, from Relays to the Stored Program Concept, 1935–1945*. Westport, CT: Greenwood Press.

Ceruzzi, Paul E. 1998. *A History of Modern Computing*. Cambridge, MA: MIT Press.

Chartier, Roger. 2007. *Inscription and Erasure: Literature and Written Culture from the Eleventh to the Eighteenth Century*. Philadelphia: University of Pennsylvania Press.

Comer, Douglas. 1997. *The Internet Book: Everything You Need to Know about Computer Networking and How the Internet Works*. Upper Saddle River, NJ: Prentice-Hall.

Copeland, B. Jack. 2006. *Colossus: The Secrets of Bletchley Park s Codebreaking Computers*. Oxford: Oxford University Press.

Cortada, James W. 1993. *The Computer in the United States: From Laboratory to Market, 1930 to 1960*. Armonk, NY: M.E. Sharpe.

Darnton, Robert. 2009. *The Case for Books: Past, Present, and Future*. New York: PublicAffairs.

Darnton, Robert, and Daniel Roche. 1989. *Revolution in Print: The Press in France, 1775–1800*. Berkeley: University of California Press in collaboration with the New York Public Library.

Diringer, David. 1982. *The Book before Printing: Ancient, Medieval, and Oriental*. New York: Dover.

Dooley, Allan C. 1992. *Author and Printer in Victorian England*. Charlottesville: University Press of Virginia.

Dubbey, J. M. 1978. *The Mathematical Work of Charles Babbage*. Cambridge: Cambridge University Press.

Engard, Nicole C. 2009. *Library Mashups: Exploring New Ways to Deliver Library Data*. Medford, NJ: Information Today.

Febvre, Lucien Paul Victor, and Henri-Jean Martin. 1976. *The Coming of the Book: The Impact of Printing 1450–1800*. London: Verso.

Finan, Christopher M. 2007. *From the Palmer Raids to the Patriot Act: A History of the Fight for Free Speech in America*. Boston: Beacon Press.

Finn, Bernard S., and Daqing Yang. 2009. *Communications under the Seas: The Evolving Cable Network and Its Implications*. Cambridge, MA: MIT Press.

Gillies, James, and R. Cailliau. 2000. *How the Web Was Born: The Story of the World Wide Web*. Oxford: Oxford University Press.

Gnanadesikan, Amalia E. 2009. *The Writing Revolution: Cuneiform to the Internet*. Chichester, UK: Wiley-Blackwell.

Goldsmith, Jack L., and Tim Wu. 2006. *Who Controls the Internet?: Illusions of a Borderless World*. New York: Oxford University Press.

Griffiths, Jeremy, and Derek Albert Pearsall. 1989. *Book Production and Publishing in Britain, 1375–1475*. Cambridge: Cambridge University Press.

Haufler, Hervie. 2003. *Codebreakers Victory: How the Allied Cryptographers Won World War II*. New York: New American Library.

Howe, Daniel Walker. 2009. *What Hath God Wrought: The Transformation of America, 1815–1848*. New York: Oxford University Press.

Hunt, Bruce J. 2010. *Pursuing Power and Light: Technology and Physics from James Watt to Albert Einstein*. Baltimore: Johns Hopkins University Press.

Hyman, Anthony. 1982. *Charles Babbage, Pioneer of the Computer*. Princeton, NJ: Princeton University Press.

Jardine, Lisa. 1996. *Worldly Goods: A New History of the Renaissance*. New York: Nan A. Talese/Doubleday.

Johns, Adrian. 2009. *Piracy: The Intellectual Property Wars from Gutenberg to Gates*. Chicago: University of Chicago Press.

Johnson, Marilyn. 2010. *This Book Is Overdue!: How Librarians and Cybrarians Can Save Us All*. New York: Harper.

Kaestle, Carl F., and Janice A. Radway. 2009. *Print in Motion: The Expansion of Publishing and Reading in the United States, 1880–1940*. Chapel Hill: University of North Carolina Press in association with the American Antiquarian Society.

Khan, B. Zorina. 2005. *The Democratization of Invention: Patents and Copyrights in American Economic Development, 1790–1920*. Cambridge: Cambridge University Press.

King, Elliot. 2010. *Free for All: The Internet s Transformation of Journalism*. Evanston, IL: Northwestern University Press.

Kirkpatrick, David. 2010. *The Facebook Effect: The Inside Story of the Company That Is Connecting the World*. New York: Simon & Schuster.

Kot, Greg. 2009. *Ripped: How the Wired Generation Revolutionized Music*. New York: Scribner.

Lastowka, F. Gregory. 2010. *Virtual Justice: The New Laws of Online Worlds*. New Haven, CT: Yale University Press.

Levmore, Saul X., and Martha Craven Nussbaum. 2010. *The Offensive Internet: Speech, Privacy, and Reputation*. Cambridge, MA: Harvard University Press.

Litman, Jessica. 2001. *Digital Copyright: Protecting Intellectual Property on the Internet*. Amherst, NY: Prometheus Books.

McLeod, Kembrew, and Peter DiCola. 2011. *Creative License: The Law and Culture of Digital Sampling*. Durham, NC: Duke University Press.

McNeely, Ian F., and Lisa Wolverton. 2008. *Reinventing Knowledge: From Alexandria to the Internet*. New York: Norton.

Mercer, David. 2006. *The Telephone: The Life Story of a Technology*. Westport, CT: Greenwood Press.

Miller, Laura J. 2006. *Reluctant Capitalists: Bookselling and the Culture of Consumption*. Chicago: University of Chicago Press.

Morozov, Evgeny. 2011. *The Net Delusion: The Dark Side of Internet Freedom*. New York: PublicAffairs.

Powers, Thomas. 1993. *Heisenberg s War: The Secret History of the German Bomb*. New York: Knopf.

Rettberg, Jill Walker. 2008. *Blogging*. Cambridge: Polity.

Ricketson, Sam, and Jane C. Ginsburg. 2006. *International Copyright and Neighbouring Rights: The Berne Convention and Beyond*. Oxford: Oxford University Press.

Runge, Laura L., and Pat Rogers. 2009. *Producing the Eighteenth-Century Book: Writers and Publishers in England, 1650–1800*. Newark: University of Delaware Press.

Ruttan, Vernon W. 2006. *Is War Necessary for Economic Growth?: Military Procurement and Technology Development*. Oxford: Oxford University Press.

Smiley, Jane. 2010. *The Man Who Invented the Computer: The Biography of John Atanasoff, Digital Pioneer*. New York: Doubleday.

Standage, Tom. 2007. *The Victorian Internet: The Remarkable Story of the Telegraph and the Nineteenth Century s On-line Pioneers*. New York: Walker.

Swade, Doron, and Charles Babbage. 2001. *The Difference Engine: Charles Babbage and the Quest to Build the First Computer*. New York: Viking.

Turkle, Sherry. 2008. *The Inner History of Devices*. Cambridge, MA: MIT Press.

Umphlett, Wiley Lee. 2006. *From Television to the Internet: Postmodern Visions of American Media Culture in the Twentieth Century*. Madison, NJ: Fairleigh Dickinson University Press.

Vandendorpe, Christian, Phyllis Aronoff, and Howard Scott. 2009. *From Papyrus to Hypertext: toward the Universal Digital Library*. Urbana: University of Illinois Press.

Vest, Charles M. 2007. *The American Research University from World War II to World Wide Web: Governments, the Private Sector, and the Emerging Meta-University*. Berkeley: Center for Studies in Higher Education, University of California Press.

Wikström, Patrik. 2009. *The Music Industry: Music in the Cloud*. Cambridge: Polity.

Winsbury, Rex. 2009. *The Roman Book: Books, Publishing and Performance in Classical Rome*. London: Duckworth.

Winseck, Dwayne Roy, and Robert M. Pike. 2007. *Communication and Empire: Media, Markets, and Globalization, 1860–1930*. Durham, NC: Duke University Press.

Index

About the Author

KARL BRIDGES is a librarian at the University of Vermont in Burlington, Vermont. He is a graduate of Franklin College, Miami University, and the University of Illinois. He is the author and/or editor of numerous articles and books including *100 Great American Novels You ve (Probably) Never Read* and *Expectations of Librarians in the 21st Century*.

Edwards Brothers Malloy
Thorofare, NJ USA
November 27, 2012